Praise for

Valley
of the
Gods

"Wolfe is an entertaining writer. . . . [She] lands on characters who are vibrant and open-minded."

—*The Atlantic*

"[Wolfe] explores the particulars of the valley itself, where youth and high-profile failure can be badges of honor, and the concentrations of wealth and intelligence are staggering. With a detached and playful tone, fly-on-the-wall Wolfe catalogs the unique habits, dress, nutrition, and mating habits of the startup class."

—*Booklist*

"Racy and fun . . . Wolfe's entertaining and intensive look inside this aspirational, transformational, and transgressive lifestyle is both celebration and cautionary tale."

—*ELLE*

"A fascinating look into the beginning stages of startups."

—*San Francisco Chronicle*

"A jauntily paced anthropological look at Northern California's techtopia. The Palo Alto semispoof is becoming a crowded genre . . . , but Wolfe, a *Wall Street Journal* reporter and former *Bloomberg Businessweek* columnist, has found relevant new eyes through which to show outsiders around."

—*Bloomberg Businessweek*

"A sharply observed, often quite funny anthropological deep dive into the strange inner workings of the Bay Area tech world."

—*Vogue*

"Captures the absurdity of this brave new world, pierces the hype but also conveys the dreams and the passions that can shape a world's economy."

—*USA Today*

"Wolfe, a *Wall Street Journal* columnist and the daughter of author Tom Wolfe, . . . chronicle[s] the peculiar and often comical mores of Silicon Valley. . . . Her narrative style is less showy than her father's, but she adopts some of his most effective literary techniques such as providing extensive descriptions of how her subjects dress, eat, exercise, and hook up."

—*National Book Review*

"Alexandra Wolfe's revealing new book, *Valley of the Gods*, offers a peek inside the privilege, power, and profligacy of Silicon Valley. Wolfe's reporting exposes the inner workings of the multibillion-dollar tech industry and also the odd behavior in which its titans indulge."

—*Town & Country*

Valley

of the

Gods

A Silicon Valley Story

Alexandra Wolfe

Simon & Schuster Paperbacks

New York   London   Toronto   Sydney   New Delhi

Simon & Schuster Paperbacks
An Imprint of Simon & Schuster, Inc.
1230 Avenue of the Americas
New York, NY 10020

First Simon & Schuster trade paperback edition January 2018

SIMON & SCHUSTER PAPERBACKS and colophon are registered
trademarks of Simon & Schuster, Inc.

For information about special discounts for bulk purchases,
please contact Simon & Schuster Special Sales
at 1-866-506-1949 or business@simonandschuster.com.

The Simon & Schuster Speakers Bureau can bring authors to your live event.
For more information or to book an event, contact the
Simon & Schuster Speakers Bureau at 1-866-248-3049
or visit our website at www.simonspeakers.com.

Interior design by Ruth Lee-Mui

Manufactured in the United States of America

1   3   5   7   9   10   8   6   4   2

Library of Congress Cataloging-in-Publication Data is available.

ISBN 978-1-4767-7894-5
ISBN 978-1-4767-7895-2 (pbk)
ISBN 978-1-4767-7896-9 (ebook)

For Mom, Dad, and Tommy

The cabin was so cosy with its little doors and windows—
A little chimney on it like a funny little hat;
A little flower-garden for the bees who wanted honey—
Now whoever, ever saw a sweeter little house than that.

Dixie Willson, *Honey Bear*

Contents

Contents

Author's Note

I first met Peter Thiel, the cofounder of PayPal, managing part-ner of Founders Fund, and first investor in Facebook, in New York at a salon at his house in 2006. He had invited a number of friends to give presentations about religion, technology, and real estate. Over the next months and years, the tech investor and I became friends, and he introduced me to the world of Silicon Valley mania. During that time, he had all sorts of ideas that most people thought were outlandish, such as building islands with libertarian principles out in the ocean, funding longevity re-search, and, more recently, financing a program to encourage stu-dents to drop out of college and start companies in Silicon Valley.

All of his ideas went against political correctness. He was a contrarian and attracted equally unique friends. Through Thiel, I discovered a whole new world of often-wacky people and ideas that didn't seem to subscribe to any set principles or social aware-ness.

His anti-university program ended up being the one that took hold in the mind of the public. Perhaps it hit at an inflection point when Americans were fed up with paying off student debt, or they couldn't find jobs after the 2007 to 2009 recession despite having degrees, but Thiel's "20 Under 20" program to grant twenty students under age twenty $100,000 to "stop out" of school started a new conversation about education.

The first year's fellows ended up being part of my window into Silicon Valley's elite and underbelly. Through their eyes, I saw a lifestyle entirely different from the East Coast's hierarchy. Through Thiel's perspective, I saw a curiosity, intelligence, and counterintuitive idealism that kept me coming back to the Bay Area more and more. This book is an attempt to capture some of the culture that attracted both me and the fellows to a place that has disrupted not only the way America does business, but also how people live their lives. In Silicon Valley, gone are the straitjacketed paths of the East Coast elite; in their place are a series of open-ended questions about which industries will be disrupted next, and which cultural configurations will supplant Old Society. Even more than a testing ground for start-ups, Silicon Valley, to me, is a larger laboratory of cultural experimentation, where the only thing that's impossible is to predict.

Prologue

It's six o'clock on a Thursday night in San Mateo County, California, at a relatively new (2009), fashionable California Craftsman–style hotel called the Rosewood Sand Hill. Out on the deck, which overlooks a bottom-lit Olympic-size pool skirted in fuchsias, huddles of lithe blondes in bright sundresses and billowy blouses perch on rancho-style woven ottomans near tablefuls of tech entrepreneurs outfitted in the techno-fabulous uniform of tight T-shirt, jeans, and tailored blazer. They're lounging under heat lamps, eating spiced popcorn and oak-grilled sliders with bottles of Sancerre wine.

This evening, however, the young blondes have competition. Every Thursday night is what regulars call Cougar Night. The cougars are women over thirty, or forty—or who dares guess—on the prowl for just the sort of delicious mortals they see spread out before them right here: one tableful after another of young techies, all of them male, most of them single, half of them innocent of a woman's wiles—and so many of them billionaires, centimillionaires, and decamillionaires that they would make any similar assembly of investment bankers and hedge fund managers cringe from the humility of inferiority and old age.

What the women, both the young and the Botoxed, have their eyes on are young pioneers who struck it rich early on when a vast, virgin terrain called the Internet started to spread across the world in the mid-1990s. Only the young and ambitious who grew up with the computer saw it for what it might become. They had absorbed the computer's digital processing early in life. To them, it didn't seem so much like a tool as it did part of their autonomic nervous systems, the part of the central nervous system that enables mammals to breathe without having to think about it. Only they could feel the boundless possibilities of the Web. Astonishingly few people born before 1970 ever *got it*, no matter how brilliant they might be in business or academia. The old boys looked at the Internet from the outside in and wondered what was the big deal. The digital age's children didn't have to look at it. It was in their innards. They were visionary puppies who realized that the Internet would become the world's first great new industry in a half century—created, developed, operated, and, more important, owned by children. It had the potential to make television and nuclear power look like relics.

It also had entry points that had never been heard of on the East Coast. Paying your dues in Silicon Valley? Out here, that meant starting as a chief executive officer of a start-up and then failing. That was step one: the glorification of starting at the top—not the bottom or the mailroom—as a founder, crashing dramatically, and then putting it on your resume as a bragging right. It was a new way of making it for those who didn't have the right pedigree. You could come from anywhere, regardless of country or degree, and there were no real steps you had to follow. The people who hit it big—and even if it was only a few billion-dollar companies—felt like they could be the everyman, or the any-nerd. It was a hopeful message, even if it was the lucky few who crowed the loudest about their improbable leap to Silicon Valley royalty.

It was also their looks. Back home, wherever they were from, a scrawny nerd with thick glasses, baggy jeans, and a T-shirt would be unlikely to score a mate. Here at Cougar Night, women were crawling on just this type of specimen.

But how could the cougars tell who was successful and who wasn't? Everyone looked the same, from the venture capitalists to the Stanford University seniors. The former may have just dyed their hair.

The scene here at the hotel reflected the industry's first glow of glamour and turned a four-mile stretch of Sand Hill Road into a destination as magnetic as Manhattan, London's Mayfair District, Paris's Champs-Élysées, Rio, Hong Kong, Las Vegas, and the Via Veneto in Rome. In short, it's the heart of the Silicon Valley, a geographical and emotional location referring to a vaguely defined fifteen-hundred-square-mile stretch beginning twenty-five miles south of San Francisco and running down the peninsula through Palo Alto and all the way to Mountain View, near San Jose.

It wasn't always this way. The area surrounding the ritzy Rosewood was a cattle farm two hundred years ago. Sand Hill Road? A cow path. A hundred years ago? The area where Facebook's sprawling campus covers acres of Menlo Park, about ten minutes from the Rosewood, was filled with fruit orchards— so many that the whole area was called the Valley of Heart's Delight.

Back then, the richest man in the valley was also an entrepreneur, but in a decidedly lower-tech field: piano manufacturing. His name was James Lick, and in the nineteenth century, he brought six hundred pounds of chocolate by Ghirardelli to San Francisco, and it was on his advice that they came to the United States and founded the Ghirardelli Chocolate Company. He also bought land. Leland Stanford, the railroad magnate and founder of Stanford University, was another deity in that era's Valley of the Gods. Stanford University was able to convince Fred Terman to leave MIT and return to Palo Alto, where he had earned undergraduate and master's degrees, to teach engineering there when most of the East Coast professors approached by the university rejected the idea of leaving what would become the Ivy League for a little-known upstart institution all the way across the country.

What they didn't know was how many other "start-ups" were going to come out of that upstart university. Bill Hewlett and Dave Packard were students there before they started what would become Hewlett-Packard—famously founded in their tiny garage, a place that is the closest thing Silicon Valley has to a temple of old. First, they did contract work, such as designing a motorized clock drive for the telescope at the Lick Observatory, named for James Lick. Finally, in 1938 they sold their resistance-capacitance audio oscillator, used for testing sound gear and priced at around $55, to the Walt Disney Company for its forthcoming animated movie *Fantasia*. Disney was their first real customer. They stopped doing contract work and became manufacturers instead.

It was Silicon Valley's first big student success story, and the first of many companies now routinely—and almost jokingly, at this point—founded in tiny garages. Halcyon Molecular, a now-defunct genome-sequencing start-up, for example, was so enamored of this "garage mystique" that even though its venture capitalist investors had given the company plenty of office space and hundreds of thousands in capital, its founders chose to work in a garage anyway.

Silicon Valley, as we think of it, didn't get its name until 1971, when California entrepreneur Ralph Vaerst named it after all the silicon chip manufacturers that had moved there. Now that valley is punctuated by the lore of its landmarks—not just garages where major companies started but also the establishments where the ideas were born. Today entire industries, aside from Internet companies, have massive bases there, such as Lockheed Martin and the National Aeronautics and Space Administration (NASA). In 1972 Kleiner Perkins (now Kleiner, Perkins, Caufield and Byers, or KPCB) became the first venture capital firm on Sand Hill Road. Now virtually all of the major venture firms have a presence there.

In this fabled land is one of the biggest concentrations of billionaires in the world. They are also the oddest bunch of billionaires: a tribe of overage boys, to a man.

From its inception, the Silicon-chic Rosewood hotel started having star-studded events that only Los Angeles and New York used to see. Back in 2011, the hotel hosted a five-hundred-person fund-raiser in its Madera restaurant for the Lucile Packard Children's Hospital, headlined by Steve Carell and Dana Carvey. Over peanut-butter-and-jelly sushi rolls and macaroni and cheese, the comedians mingled with some of the foremost philanthropists in the country, including chairwomen Anne Lawler and Elizabeth Dunlevie, wives of prominent venture capitalists. And these celebrities arrived only weeks after others—from President Barack Obama, to Katy Perry, to Snoop Dogg—had made a point of passing through Palo Alto to pay homage to Silicon Valley's boy CEOs.

Still, even years ago, a hopping power scene in Silicon Valley would have been considered an oxymoron. Casual was king, and engineering, emperor. Today it's hard to keep the money out. Now there are tech barons such as Mark Zuckerberg—thirty-two years old, worth $35 billion after he went public with Facebook; Jeremy Stoppelman of Yelp; Dustin Moskovitz of Asana; Charlie Cheever of Quora; LinkedIn cofounder Reid Hoffman, at forty-nine, ancient for a founder; Sergey Brin, the Russian-born entrepreneur who cofounded Google in 1998 when he was twenty-five; and, above all, Peter Thiel, who cofounded what would become PayPal the same year at age thirty-one. Most of them are regulars at Madera restaurant. PayPal was the Internet's first bank, giving online commerce badly needed rigor and rules. When eBay bought PayPal in 2002, Thiel rolled his share of the money into a hedge fund. Then he invested in Facebook, helping it to become a real company when it was nothing but Zuckerberg's hopeful lark.

Thiel made nearly $2 billion when Facebook sold for upward of $100 billion in an initial public offering, or IPO, ten years later. By then, he had invested in over a dozen more start-ups and started a hedge fund of his own, called Clarium Capital Management. He had also begun thinking of what the new industry and information technology in general could do for a society. He was its first philosopher. He's now known as the godfather of the PayPal Mafia, which includes Hoffman and Stoppelman, who went on to found many of Silicon Valley's splashiest tech companies.

Today's uber-nerds are like the robber barons of the industrial revolution whose steel and automobile manufacturing capabilities changed entire industries.* But instead of massive factories and mills, they're doing it with little buttons. Actually, buttons would be an overstatement. They're doing it with a tip of a finger. With a single tap of the Uber app, millions of users have disrupted the transportation industry in America. Now hailing a cab is an anachronism. You might as well ride a covered wagon. As for dining, in a growing number of cities around the world, apps and sites such as OpenTable and Yelp make sampling new places—or discovering them in ads—passé.

For the first time, tech titans are celebrities themselves, and

---

* "Robber Barons and Silicon Sultans," *The Economist*, January 3, 2015.

their lives have become objects of fascination. The tech boom has not only launched new media, it has also created a new social order, one with an anti-"society" aesthetic that has taken on a singular style. Here more than 5 percent of the residents are millionaires and help make up the wealthiest 1 percent of the country. Since 2010, the resurgence of tech has brought two hundred thousand new jobs to the area. In the last year, the price of the average single-family residence in Palo Alto—home to eight newly minted billionaires, including Zuckerberg and Sergey Brin—rose to $2.5 million. Many of those homes were bought with profits of payouts from the first boom, such as those earned by early employees of Google and the technology company Oracle. Twenty more billionaires live in the surrounding towns, and their off-the-charts successes have set the tone for an area of extremes: extreme health, extreme comfort, and, of course, extreme wealth.

It's the last extreme—wealth—that isn't outwardly detectable, and that's the key to Silicon Valley style. "The richest person in the room is often wearing flip-flops and a hoodie," says entrepreneur David Llorens. The hoodie becomes the symbol of Mark Zuckerberg, the richest of the new breed. He's thirty-two and looks twenty. Youth is a *must* for the new breed; they go to great lengths to appear young. They have no interest in society in the old sense of dignified New York, Boston, Philadelphia Society—or even San Francisco Society, forty miles away. It's as if

San Francisco doesn't exist. The transistor and the microchip and the Internet were all created by midwesterners and westerners. To the pioneers, inventors William Shockley and Robert Noyce, eastern ways seemed decadent.

From the moment the valley wakes up, the day unfolds much like it does for the students on the nearby Stanford campus. Most wealthy tech founders do not rise under twenty-foot ceilings or stumble into marble bathrooms with lofty bay windows to brush their teeth. Unlike the storied mansions of Greenwich, Connecticut, and Long Island, the moguls of Silicon Valley's houses are often inversely proportional in size to the year they made their money. Whereas older billionaires such as Oracle founder Larry Ellison live in gated compounds along Woodside's Mountain Home Road or Atherton's Park Lane, younger entrepreneurs, many of whom have already sold their companies for hundreds of millions, increasingly stay in their first apartment or that same sentimental start-up garage they moved to after Stanford. They witnessed the housing bubble firsthand, are often single, and prefer to invest in companies.

They may look like they live in dorms, but they reside in homes that cost $35,000 ten years ago and now sell for $2 million. The cattle farms that existed in the 1850s on the road between Cupertino and downtown San Jose are no longer full of flower petals and fruit but of frozen yogurt and cereal bars. It's the dormification of acres of land. Ironically, many of the residents seem to find college inconsequential.

It was Google that first defined the social identity that companies gave their employees. Engineers go to grad school at Google and Facebook and become perennial students. They keep wearing the student uniform and often start companies with their friends from college. From the picnic benches up and down Palo Alto's University Avenue to entrepreneurs' backyard barbecues outside one-story row houses in Sunnyvale, Silicon Valley is a place of eternal freshman herds.

As the area's wealth increases, so do the lengths that entrepreneurs will go to hide it. "Beverly Hills is great, but that's not us," says former Palo Alto mayor Sid Espinosa. "We're not flashy and glitzy—and we don't strive to be. In fact, it's antithetical to our culture." Katrina Garnett, the dashing forty-three-year-old former tech exec says she's seen an increase in requests for building permits to build down, not up. The number of elaborate basement expansions has skyrocketed in recent years. When someone as successful as Reid Hoffman decides to stay in the same one-bedroom apartment after making $3 billion in a single week, it sets an anti-ostentatious tone.

In the morning, entrepreneurs walk down Palo Alto's oak-tree-lined streets to offices atop retail stores and restaurants or drive their Priuses to cafes such as Fraîche for cups of Blue Bottle artisanal drip coffee, homemade oatmeal, and local Clover milk yogurt with candied walnuts and berries. Bicycles fill University Avenue, some ridden by commuters, others by company cycling teams wearing matching Day-Glo jackets.

Farther from Palo Alto, where Sand Hill Road turns into Portola Road, early-morning bikers race through Portola Valley while their wives ride horses at Portola Farms. The fitness expert of choice is CrossFit, whose trainers take techies cycling up winding Old La Honda Road. One of the tour notes is the former home of the late Ken Kesey, the author and hippy/psychedelic movement leader. But it's only that: a tour note. In 1964 Kesey created a commune, the Merry Pranksters, at his house. Then he led them on a cross-country tour proselytizing their acid-fueled religion in a 1939 International Harvester school bus (and flogging the imminent publication of his new book, *Sometimes a Great Notion*).

Offhand, it's hard to think of two more opposite types of literate young men. The techies' one true obsession is work. The Pranksters' one true obsession was *not* working, which Kesey called "moving off of dead center," and taking hallucinogens until, as he also put it, you "junked it out through the other side." Today the techies drive their electric Tesla roadsters to work down El Camino Real, the thoroughfare that connects all the different Silicon Valley cities of Atherton, Woodside, Mountain View, and Palo Alto. Women who work take breaks between conference calls to go shopping at the Stanford Shopping Center, full of high-end boutiques. The Left Coast Ladies Who Lunch do so over Clif Bars while walking the Dish, the popular hiking trail on Stanford property—and "Ladies" means over age twenty-nine. In a place where the fashion is function and the affectation is efficiency, Silicon Valley's new lifestyle is not for the weary.

Instead of socialites, Silicon Valley has technolites. Far from chairing the charity ball, the modus operandi of the upwardly mobile female is to match her hobby with PayPal, sell jewelry or embroidered dog beds or pastel belts online, launch a website, and then anoint herself CEO. She, along with female power execs, wears the understated uniform of Lanvin flats, Majestic tees, James Jeans, and cozy cashmere sweaters. Already reminiscent of West Palm Beach's City Center, the Stanford Shopping Center's palm-tree-covered walkways have a casual, woodsy feel, and offshoots lead to gourmet farm-stand-meets-food-shop cafes.

At the Village Pub in Woodside, the tech execs scarf down thick pub burgers with fries and duck-and-lentil salads, eating fast so they can run back out to their Priuses in under an hour. It is a place where socializing and networking are interchangeable, and the greatest proof of upward mobility is dwindling time. "The social aspect is not a vehicle for us to get anywhere," says Garnett, the founder of My Little Swans, an online platform for luxury travel. "Here it's all about having money and no time," she explains. Garnett, a petite blonde, is also an investor and former software engineer. "If anyone talks about their golf handicap, you'd look at them and say, 'I'd never invest in you because you spend too much time on the golf course.'" Instead, less time-consuming passions persist, such as collecting art and wine. Garnett says that she and her husband acquire art because it doesn't require as much time as, say, golfing all day would. As for cars, "Do we all own Ferraris? Yes," says Garnett. "But would we drive it into a start-up's parking lot? No." She laughs. "We'd drive the Prius and keep the Ferrari in the garage."

In San Francisco, most children of the elite families go to one of a handful of private schools, but in Silicon Valley, most tech parents, including venture capitalist Vinod Khosla, send their kids to the alternative Nueva School (and so did the late Steve Jobs). There students focus thematically on, say, ancient Greece or American history one semester at a time, rather than on traditional subject categories.

Working women have their centers of power too: from Facebook chief operating officer Sheryl Sandberg's women's salons to the speakeasy basement parties hosted by venture capitalist Aileen Lee.

If the early wave of billion-dollar companies such as Google and Facebook brought about a new social identity, it's the billionaires themselves who have launched a movement. From Tesla CEO Elon Musk to Peter Thiel, the tech titans at the helm of these enterprises have created an aspirational culture of optimistic young graduates who want to change the world, not just make money. Unlike wannabe Wall Street worker bees whose first stop from New York's Penn Station is Thomas Pink or Charles Tyrwhitt for shirts, then Tourneau for a watch, and finally Tiffany for their monogrammed belt buckle, the only outward signs of tech success are laptops and ideas. The billionaires themselves dress indistinguishably from Stanford students. They drive around in jeans and fleeces, just perhaps in faster cars. The other distinguishing characteristic their particular fantasy evokes, more than the typical West Coast daydream of being a Hollywood producer or director, is freedom. As a tech entrepreneur, there is no studio head to report to, no investment banking board, and no shareholders unless their company IPOs—which basically means retirement, at least from that particular venture.

It's a tether-free life that has permeated Palo Alto, and it is visible on every street. Coffee shops such as Coupa Café in Palo Alto and Hobee's in Sunnyvale typically host diners and their laptops for hours on end. All of them are trying to come up with the next Facebook and honestly think they can. It's a place where risk aversion doesn't exist; what Silicon Valley lacks in nightlife excitement it makes up for with its day jobs' thrills, most of which entail gambling every day on what the next big idea will be.

New technology is always present: for instance, now an increasing number of restaurants from Palo Alto to San Francisco International Airport have iPads replacing waiters.

After a long day of coding, eating, and exercising, nights out end early. Palo Alto is dark after ten o'clock, save for the rows of lit windows where engineers are still working well into the next morning. For most, though, they're saving energy for the weekend ahead. Google, Airbnb, and Twitter all have fitness and yoga classes. Palo Alto's retail space is punctuated by fitness storefronts run often by wives of successful area financiers, such as Dianne Giancarlo's the 3rd Door, a now-shuttered private training club where clients could come by for thirty-minute "body slams" designed to fit in with the start-up schedule.

The excesses crammed into such little leisure time are often experiential. For example, Mint founder Aaron Patzer doesn't buy big houses; instead, he takes "epic" trips. Over Pingg.com, an invitation app, Patzer said he and thirty other entrepreneurs, including his friends AdBrite founder Phil Kaplan and Tesla's Elon Musk, were organizing an event two hours north where they would all bring their own equipment, including zip lines for rappelling.

Patzer spent his days off, before leaving Intuit, working toward his pilot's license. The weekend before, he and Barney Pell, founder of the semantic search company Powerset, had gone for a ride on Pell's new dirigible to test its lunar landing radar. The boy was not kidding. If Silicon Valley's newly minted millionaires keep up the velocity, a few weeks, months, years from now, they'll land on the moon. Palo Alto has become the promised land, and even more than in Ken Kesey's heyday, *crazy* is a compliment.

In Silicon Valley, arriving to the area without a pedigree has no stigma. As of 2014, every day, hundreds of people were arriving there, from the East Coast, Europe, Asia, all wanting to create the best new company—or at least make money off it. They gravitate to the area where their specialty, or basic skill, lies. Hard-core engineering and enterprise software companies are based mostly in the southern valley, in Cupertino and Mountain View. Then there's biotech, in Mountain View and slowly creeping up to Menlo Park. Consumer Internet companies now rule certain areas of San Francisco, such as the booming Mission District, where Twitter has taken over entire city blocks—and those are San Francisco city blocks, not the measly blocks of Manhattan, the former home of the American business elite.

These days, being a part of a place where entirely new industries have disrupted the old—all by children, and aspiring children—is too tempting to pass up. The only question is: Once you get to the promised land, how do you make it there?

1

Asperger's Chic

John Burnham wanted to mine asteroids. He had always been a little bit different. Instead of reading school textbooks or his summer reading list, he read Plato, Aristotle, and a modern-day "neoreactionary" thinker who goes by the pen name Mencius Moldbug. A self-declared libertarian and "self-directed learner," motivated to study on his own, Burnham felt like he didn't need teachers to tell him what to do. He was a terribly behaved student.

By the spring semester of his senior year of high school in 2011, John had been rejected or wait-listed from all ten colleges he applied to except the University of Massachusetts, just over ten miles away from where he lived in Newton, Massachusetts. He didn't really care, though, since the idea of enduring another four years of dull lectures and drearier tests was less than appealing. It was a distraction from what he had always wanted to do, which was to go into space—and reap trillions of dollars from the valuable minerals that existed in asteroids.

Burnham wasn't delusional. He knew what he was talking about. While most of his classmates read *Tess of the d'Urbervilles* and *The Great Gatsby,* he was researching nickel, cobalt, and platinum on S-type (silacaceous) asteroids. With bright blue eyes, blond hair, and a seemingly permanent smirk, he was popular with girls and distracted himself with brief high school flirtations, but John still had plenty of time for his loftier interests. As he procrastinated doing the homework assignments he found pointless, he scoured the Web, stumbling across bloggers whose ideas were at least more interesting than those of his current teachers.

His favorite was called *Unqualified Reservations,* written by the reactionary blogger Mencius Moldbug, whose real name is Curtis Yarvin. An engineer living in Silicon Valley, Yarvin described himself in his blog's "About Me" section with the words "stubbornness and disrespect." Burnham was hooked.

One night, when John was up reading Patri Friedman's blog, he came upon a new posting announcing a call for applications to a fellowship called 20 Under 20. Sponsored by the Thiel Foundation, it offered twenty students under twenty years old $100,000 to drop out of school, forgo college for the duration of the fellowship, and start their own companies. Drop out of school? Burnham didn't have to be convinced. He wasn't sure what his mother and father, a Congregationalist minister and a financial investor, respectively, would think of the idea, but he was curious to find out more.

The Thiel Foundation turned out to be the charitable arm of an empire belonging to Peter Thiel, founder and chairman of the Founders Fund, a major Silicon Valley venture capital firm that had invested in companies such as Spotify, the music streaming subscription service, and the ride-sharing service Lyft. Burnham clicked from article to article: from the *Forbes* magazine piece that described Thiel's chef and butler to the *Fortune* article calling him one of best investors in the country.

In 2011 Thiel was a youthful forty-three. He had just announced the fellowship in fall 2010 at a conference called Tech-Crunch Disrupt. The conference was sponsored by TechCrunch, a website dedicated to news and gossip about the valley, and also served as a tech company directory, listing founders, investors, and financing rounds. At first, Thiel's announcement was a way to call attention to what he considered the waste of time and money spent on a college education. He also railed against the political correctness he thought universities propagated. By selecting a group of high school students who would otherwise have gone to four-year institutions to start life early, he hoped to prove that the college model was outdated. Burnham was already familiar with some of Thiel's projects and often outlandish ideas. While he ran his hedge fund, Clarium, or funded Silicon Valley start-ups by day at the Founders Fund, Thiel also had a penchant for pursuing original causes, no matter how crazy they seemed.

One of these was the Seasteading Institute, a project to create a libertarian community at sea, where people could buy a man-made island and govern themselves. The head of the Seasteading Institute was a then thirty-four-year-old former Google engineer named Patri Friedman, grandson of the economist Milton Friedman. Patri's ideas regularly popped up on Moldbug's blog, and vice versa. Burnham often read Friedman's libertarian musings, and when he saw the fellowship advertised on his site as well, the seventeen-year-old knew he had to apply.

The application asked questions such as "What do you believe that no one else does?" Burnham had a ready answer: just about everything. While on the surface he seemed like a typical high school senior, with a cheery demeanor and outgoing personality, it was as though he lived on another plane that hovered over everyone else his age. His mind was up in the sky.

As Burnham saw it, the application wasn't only an entrée to Silicon Valley but also a way to reach a farther frontier: space. If anyone could help him get there, it was this Thiel character, with the big ideas, contrarian outlook, and a willingness to back crazy concepts. Winning the fellowship would present a way out of even more years of inculcation of an educational canon that had never made sense to him, as well as a chance to focus full-time on these bigger-picture problems that he would soon hear as a steady refrain throughout Silicon Valley as "changing the world." John didn't just want to be a Thiel Fellow. He *needed* to become one. Otherwise he was going to backpack around Europe instead.

In Silicon Valley, he thought, people might take seriously what his friends and teachers ridiculed back in Boston. There, they too might believe they could live on Mars someday. Out west, in the promised land, they wouldn't look at him like he was crazy when he talked about the money that could be made from mining asteroids.

So he started writing his answers. Why did we need to go to space? "At the core of the Earth is the most unbelievable mother lode of heavy elements," he explained. The problem was accessing them. "Dense elements have over the eons sunk into the depths of the Earth." Burnham had long wanted to figure out a way to dredge up at least some of these. He didn't understand why no one had done so already.

He thought more about that application's first question. While most people didn't think we urgently needed to get to space, most people also believed in a set of basic beliefs that he didn't. Take democracy, for one. Why, he wondered, did everyone believe in it so blindly? Instead, John thought, democracy was really oligarchy: government by a select few. He'd borrowed this idea from Moldbug's blog and then looked for the same concept in Plato. "Plato is magnificent," he said matter-of-factly.

Some of his political views had been informed by reading about the history of the French Revolution and the writings of Edmund Burke, an Irish-born political thinker and member of the British Parliament in the eighteenth century. Burnham grappled with the idea of how monarchy and democracy are similar, about how they are both the rule of the many by the few.

He wondered why none of his friends asked the questions he did and why his teachers were always telling him his interruptions were bothersome. He didn't think he was all that different from the people he read, only the people he met. Was he too influenced by these blogs, by the opinions of others? he wondered.

The next question was one that Burnham had been thinking about for as long as he could remember: "How would you change the world?"

He had researched a number of asteroids. He didn't understand why so many people had been against NASA's spending more than $224 million on its unmanned mission to the asteroid Eros 433 in 1996, for example, when he felt certain that the platinum and gold floating up in that asteroid would be worth trillions. The spacecraft took four years to reach the solid space rock, then orbited it for another twelve months, gathering essential data.

Why hadn't technology improved? Why couldn't a payload of 487 kilograms of spacecraft, sensors, and electronics be stored on Eros 433 for less than hundreds of millions of dollars? he wondered. He had studied every aspect of Eros. The wind there was solar wind. The hill was shallow, and the wind as strong, so why couldn't they use solar sails to move it? he asked.

Burnham figured the only expensive part would be getting up there. He had heard about Virgin Group founder Richard Branson's space tourism company Virgin Galactic, but wasn't particularly excited about it—and that was before one of their spaceships crashed. He saw it as a vacation for only the wealthy. And the teenager had high hopes for SpaceX, a rocket company founded by Elon Musk, a friend of Thiel's and a cofounder of PayPal, as well as Blue Origin, a space exploration company funded by Amazon founder Jeff Bezos.

If the government wasn't doing anything about it, at least these guys were, he figured. But what none of them was doing was developing a robot to mine the asteroids. Burnham wanted to make that happen. "I don't think this should actually be terribly impossible," he wrote on his Thiel fellow application. All the robot would have to do was dig.

Burnham figured that the robots would excavate the minerals

and then bring them back to Earth to be processed. Eventually they could be processed in space, but he thought it should probably happen on Earth first even though some of the minerals might be destroyed in the process. He had already thought about how to get these chunks of rock from Earth's orbit to its surface. Maybe foils, parachutes, or balloons could work, he mused. The chunks would have to be small enough to burn up in the atmosphere, and their orbit would have to degrade into the ocean. "I'd hate to cause another Tunguska event over a major city, or even a small town," he said in his application. "Bad publicity." He was referring to what happened over Siberia in 1908, when a large asteroid believed to weigh 220 million pounds and traveling 33,500 miles per hour disintegrated five miles up in the sky, setting off an explosion as powerful as the atomic bomb later dropped on Hiroshima, Japan—times 185.

Someone must have considered this idea already, Burnham thought to himself. Maybe at SpaceX? He wanted to meet whoever these people were and be part of this discovery, or perhaps it would be a race, if there were a lot of people working on it. "The first one there becomes the next Standard Oil," he thought. "In any case, this is the easiest way that I can see to fulfill one of the dreams of the last fifty years of space exploration: to make space profitable."

But to John, the most exciting part of space was the idea of a new frontier, or "the next frontier," he said. "Space is big. I bet that it's big enough so that if a group of people want to create a society that completely contravenes every legal and moral principle of the United States, they'll be free to find a place to do it." This place would be a new Plymouth, Massachusetts; or a new Jamestown, Virginia; or Salt Lake City or San Francisco. "Space allows for people to fulfill that primal urge to pioneer," he wrote.

When Burnham told his parents about his desire to apply to the Thiel Fellowship, they were supportive. They had long wondered what to do with their unconventional genius. They couldn't reconcile the subjects and ideas that interested him—far more advanced than anyone else's his age—with a known academic track.

Burnham's parents thought it might be possible for him to learn something in college but that he'd likely learn more outside the system. His father, Stephen Burnham, told the *New York Times*, "I would say in four years there's a big opportunity cost there if you could be out starting your career doing something that could change the world."

John's parents couldn't get him excited about any age-appropriate institution, and he didn't want to leave his education to his online heroes, such as Friedman or Moldbug. Here was a fellowship run by a man with a real track record. Somehow it seemed to fit with their child's uncanny musings and excite him.

He could be the harbinger of a new kind of prodigy: the self-directed learner whose superior skill set demanded a new kind of plan not yet available on the ivy-covered East Coast track. The track of private school to boarding school to college wasn't working, despite their son's apparent brilliance. Here was a respectable option, at least.

A few months later, among Burnham's rejection letters from college came an acceptance to the Thiel Fellowship's final round. To him, it was the closest he'd come to getting to space. To the Burnhams, it was some kind of direction—the opposite of what they feared he'd find at the University of Massachusetts, where he would be even more bored than he was in high school.

Burnham had already been screened twice on the phone; first by his blogging hero Patri Friedman, who was helping Thiel organize the fellowship and choose the finalists. "We talked a fair bit about asteroid mining," Burnham remembered excitedly. He then spoke with Danielle Strachman, the Thiel Foundation staffer in charge of providing a structure for what the fellows would do once they got to California.

By that point, both Burnham and his parents found the possibility of winning the fellowship even more selective than getting into an Ivy League institution. When they met the other finalists, most had been accepted to prestigious universities such as Harvard, Yale, and Princeton. They chose the fellowship instead. The list of finalists leaked out, making them suddenly objects of intense interest from media outlets around the country. As John said to the *Times*, "[The fellowship] is giving them that opportunity even though their personalities and characters don't quite fit the academic mold."

The final rounds took place in spring 2011 at the Hyatt Regency Hotel in San Francisco. To get to the subterranean conference room in the lower lobby of the behemoth building, parents and finalists walked aimlessly through the cavernous space, asking staffers to point them to the Thiel Foundation's event. When they finally found the small room, they encountered Burnham and nearly forty other finalists who were nervously walking back and forth up and down a narrow hall outside the room where they would be giving brief presentations. They whispered in huddles outside, wondering who everyone was.

After a tense few minutes, they filed into the room to see Thiel himself standing up at a podium, and an audience of casually dressed San Francisco techies who would be their mentors, if they were selected. That March day marked the last round of the selection process. Following the candidates' presentations, everyone attended a reception at Thiel's house. Later, audience members would fill out forms ranking the fellows. A few weeks later, the top twenty would be picked.

Thiel has an angular, expressive face, and a direct demeanor. That day, like most days, he wore tailored jeans, a polo shirt, and sneakers. He was used to public speaking, and did so in crisp, clear sentences, with no added emphasis on his many controversial points. He presented forgoing a college education as entirely logical.

He, like many of the people in the room, from the tech execs to the aspiring fellows, weren't the kind of people you would find schmoozing at Manhattan cocktail parties. They weren't socially at ease and didn't like small talk. Some were awkward. If they even went to a party, they much preferred talking to one good friend, or someone they thought was uniquely or esoterically intelligent. Social barometers really meant nothing.

After speeches, Thiel was sometimes asked if he thought there was a high percentage of people with Asperger's syndrome in Silicon Valley. He dismissed the disorder and its traits as the only ways that smooth-talking socially adept types could describe people they couldn't understand. He doesn't even believe in the spectrum, or the range of disorders that could be variations on the social impairments symptomatic of autism or Asperger's. In fact, under the *DSM-5*, Asperger's syndrome and autism spectrum disorder are shown as far more than social impairments—they can produce learning disabilities, mental retardation, anxiety disorder, and Tourette syndrome, among other ailments.

But in Silicon Valley, that behavior was Asperger's Chic. When faced with choosing two engineers with the same skill set, employers would often take the one with the stutter over the smooth talker, any day. Some employers unofficially sought out socially awkward recruits. They tended to be more productive, recruiters felt.

Thiel was never a fan of cocktail party culture. He didn't like talking about mundane topics such as the weather, or vacations, just to make conversation. His reticence on those subjects led people to think he was awkward. Thiel was certainly capable of talking about the weather; he just didn't understand why he needed to waste time doing so. Talking about a subject that interested him, Thiel was as charismatic as they came, much like John Burnham. In the first few minutes, the teenager would be outgoing and energetic, but after ten more minutes it became clear that he didn't particularly want to change topics or talk about someone else's day, for that matter.

It was a personality that might not get a future programmer or engineer into one of Harvard's exclusive social clubs, like the Fly Club or the Spee Club, elite members organizations that were the school's version of fraternities, but to the programmers, what would *those* people ever become? What was the use of social graces if it couldn't help solve an engineering problem or write the code for a new company? *They* had an idealism that some sense of social awareness might have censored. In a way, it was scoffing at what *those others* have to say: those weather-asking chatterers who couldn't understand the complexity of thinking out of bounds.

That afternoon, Thiel was explaining enthusiastically that young people would do better to educate themselves as opposed to pay to enroll in a four-year institution. "All great entrepreneurs have a passion about education and self-education," he projected to the group of fifty or so professors, entrepreneurs, investors, and friends in the Hyatt conference room. "It's never too early to begin." Higher education, he said, was a distraction from thinking about what to actually do in life. "You lose sight of a plan and intention about the future," he added.

The investors in the room were already convinced. Most had succeeded by thinking unconventionally and veering off one track or another, whether it was dropping out of a PhD program or turning down a job at a bank or consulting company. None showed signs of ever having worked at a giant corporation such as Goldman Sachs or Morgan Stanley. As for the applicants, they were just happy to be in Thiel's audience. At this point, they hadn't really thought about what this new kind of plan would entail, where they would live, how they would get there, or even what specifically they would do.

Thiel then told an anecdote from the early days at Facebook. He said that when Mark Zuckerberg was offered $1 billion to sell the company in 2006, the founder and CEO refused because he still had plans for the company in the future. Facebook is now valued at over $100 billion. If he'd sold out too soon, he'd be just an another engineer, albeit with a second home or two.

"You don't have to be dogmatic, but you have to have a plan," Thiel stressed, adding that today students saw going to college as a path to having career options—but after the recession, those options were increasingly less available. And it was a vicious cycle. Just going to college was supposed to give students more opportunities, until he or she went into a tracked career, such as banking or consulting. Those jobs weren't the final goal, however. They were just the next steps to having even more options, whatever those options were. Maybe they could someday enroll in some kind of graduate school, the function of which was to offer still more options. The recession, however, had pruned the option tree and had left students without plans but hopes of optimizing on ever-expanding choices that often led back to living in their parents' houses. "Any plan is better than no plan," Thiel said.

The audience looked like it had already internalized his advice. From Dr. Aubrey de Grey, a British Cambridge University graduate with a nearly two-foot-long beard, to Patri Friedman, with his Fives sneakers and goatee, no one looked as though he or she still subscribed to any institution resembling the East Coast elite. Professor de Grey, who was bent on "curing" aging, was on hand to help choose the final twenty, while a handful of the other mentors had already helped screen applications. Their influence soon became clear: at least half the students onstage put forth ideas in the science or biotech space, among them Laura Deming, a New Zealand–born prodigy who'd joined MIT's research lab to study longevity at age *twelve*, and British-born James Proud, who ended his biotech pitch with the line "Even those who want to get to heaven don't want to die to get there." Others had trendier ideas—for instance, involving social media or e-commerce—such as Paul Gu, who later transitioned to a personal lending start-up.

When the finalists had applied back in December 2010, the foundation made it clear that it didn't want another social networking site. "Maybe another Tumblr blog will change the world. But it sure isn't going to put someone on Mars," said Jonathan Cain, the slim, bespectacled president of the Thiel Foundation. Cain was a Yale graduate who used to be a speechwriter for George W. Bush's secretary of health and human services, but had since seen the Silicon Valley light. He started working on political donations—mostly to libertarian and Republican causes—for Thiel until he moved over to his philanthropic side to fund unusual projects in the charity world. He didn't intend to support big city zoos or museums or hosted galas to save polar bears or Venice. Instead, he was supposed to look for what was already good or promising and fund it to make it better, such as brilliant scientists working on faster ways to sequence DNA.

"We're not looking for the next Facebook—we're looking for people who are thinking two to ten years beyond what the rest of the world thinks is possible today," said Cain. It was a tall order, one so high that even the teenagers filling out the application, most of whom were still in high school, would have to stretch to come up with an idea at all. But then, that was how many Silicon Valley start-ups had begun. The foundation had selected these forty finalists out of four hundred applicants based on how originally and compellingly they had answered the questions, such as what the world's biggest problems are and why their idea "simply cannot wait." The forty had proposed ideas that the foundation considered counterintuitive. Those who weren't selected applied with hackneyed social media company ideas, or copies of what already existed. Basically, the forty they picked were oddballs. Or in other words, they'd fit in out here.

Soon after Thiel's speech, the finalists began their presentations and came up to the podium one after the other. Some were barely tall enough to clear it. John Burnham was among the first. While some of the first few finalists sputtered and stuttered, giving jargon-heavy presentations with esoteric technical names, there was no mistaking what Burnham was talking about. From the moment he strode to the podium, looked up at the audience, and began speaking, it was as if he were channeling a friendlier Howard Roark—the uncompromising young protagonist in Ayn Rand's 1943 novel *The Fountainhead*. John seemed so unaware of how outrageous his idea was that he said it almost conversationally: "I am going to mine asteroids." His determined diction, much like Thiel's, made it clear that he was not joking. Nobody laughed. Burnham then explained that his goal was to develop space industry technologies to mine asteroids and other planetary bodies such as comets for gold and platinum. He listed in exacting detail the compounds and elements he hoped to find there. "There are hundreds of billions of dollars out there in the universe," he said, "and I plan to find it." Burnham practically got a standing ovation.

Laura Deming, a striking seventeen-year-old half-Asian wunderkind, looked like a schoolgirl gone bad, but with her rapid speech and frantic gesticulations, she sounded more mad scientist. Waves of unkempt, long, black hair framed her porcelain face, and her tall, lithe body was covered in an untucked Oxford shirt, black miniskirt, and stockings, along with a pair of hulking black combat boots that swallowed her shapely calves. Her tiny figure and doll-like mouth made her serious, deadpan voice surprising. Far from dainty and meek, Deming slashed her frail arms left and right like a conductor angry with her orchestra.

Having spent the last four years, since age twelve, working in gerontology labs, she said she was frustrated by the lack of sufficient funds for immortality research. With a Thiel Fellowship, she would create her own private equity firm to fund antiaging breakthroughs. "I want to disrupt the current research paradigm by changing the incentives embedded in today's traditional funding structures," she said. It wouldn't be the craziest thing she'd done, either. Homeschooled in New Zealand, Deming finished high school at fourteen and enrolled at MIT as the school's youngest sophomore.

James Proud, a small, stocky eighteen-year-old high school

graduate from South London, also stood out among the crowd. He looked about ten years old, but when he spoke, his deep voice and British accent made him sound as though he were fifty. His presentation came later. He had already moved to Palo Alto even though he hadn't been accepted to the program yet. James, who'd been coding in his bedroom through most of high school, had told his parents he didn't want to go to college well before the Thiel Fellowship was even an option. He did want to go to music concerts, however, but couldn't find a single website that listed all the shows he wanted to see. So his idea was to create GigLocator, which would aggregate shows big and small on a single app.

After the presentations, the fellows and their parents went to Thiel's big bayfront house in the Marina District of San Francisco for a reception. Investors hoping to be mentors to Burnham surrounded the young finalist. He soaked in the attention and pitched one venture capitalist after the other with the poise of a seasoned actor on the red carpet. With many in attendance already invested in the private rocket company SpaceX, the brainchild of Elon Musk, they wanted to know if Burnham's theory could really work. Barney Pell, the founder of Powerset and later the commercial space company Moon Express, peppered the teen with questions. Although John was engaging, he, like many of the already successful entrepreneurs at the reception, didn't ask many questions of others. It was his show, and he was happy to be on display.

"You have an asteroid you send into orbit, right?" he explained to the attentive group. "You have to be careful when you send it into orbit."

"How are you going to send it into orbit?" asked Laura Deming's father, John.

"Well, I have to send it into the orbit I want," he said.

"But you're still not answering the question," said Mr. Deming. "When can this actually happen?"

"When the world's not ready for your idea, there's an easy solution," said Burnham. "Wait." It was an answer he had given before, one meant to be funny and tidy at the same time. He gave them a little smirk, as they had no response, or a better idea.

A white-haired mentor standing nearby asked John what he thought of SpaceX. "I hear Elon Musk is against asteroid mining," said the man. "I hear he's ignoring the asteroid question and focusing on lunar landings to start with."

"I don't know why Elon Musk would be against asteroids," Burnham replied. "Because their mission is to get to Mars, and to get to Mars, you need asteroids." No one argued with him. He knew so many esoteric astronomical phrases that there was little common knowledge that could refute him.

"Believe me, it will be like the gold rush," Burnham said excitedly of his idea to mine asteroids for valuable materials. "There's an asteroid called Eros," he explained to the circle surrounding him. "The gold and platinum there are worth at least a hundred billion dollars. It is like rocket fuel.

"Asteroid mining will not only open up space but will also be profitable," he continued, as if it was incomprehensible that no one had ever thought of it before. Somehow the eighteen-year-old's lofty proclamations came off as endearing. It was a trait that made you root for him. Looking at his flashing blue eyes, eager expression, and ever-present smile, and listening to his command of his material, you could imagine yourself reading his name in the headlines one day and thinking, "I knew him back when."

The billion-dollar company that would "change the world" was the Silicon Valley version of Wall Street's "number": the figure that bankers bandied about to describe how much money they planned to make. But here the affectation was noble aspiration. The idea of creating something that took over an industry or influenced the future was something that some of the guests in the room, such as Luke Nosek, who'd helped cofound PayPal, or Sean Parker, who'd founded Napster, had done. For them, it wasn't a stretch to talk about it in literal terms.

After all, when Thiel declared in 1998, "I'm going to create an online currency," PayPal, he did. Here announcing you would end aging or mine asteroids gave you entry. The finalists, all intelligent beyond their years and maniacally focused on their projects, also obsessively believed in their ideas in a larger-than-life way. For each, asking about the lunch or dinner would have elicited monosyllabic answers, but asking what company they hoped to found would start a soliloquy. Depending on the listener, the speech turned into either a four-hour debate and possibly a new start-up, or a glance toward the nearest exit.

A few weeks later, Burnham and his parents were on their way to New York. They would be having lunch at Aureole, a cavernous three-star restaurant that mostly served as a throwback to a white-gloved East Coast luxury that had been largely lost since the recession.

Burnham had just found out he'd won a fellowship, and he was thrilled. The lunch was for fellows in the area who had been chosen but hadn't yet accepted. It was the Thiel Foundation's campaign to put their parents at ease.

Just before noon on a crisp spring Saturday, tourist patrons at Aureole looked up surprised to see a pack of teenagers flooding into a private room behind the hostess stand. It was an empty, formal space that looked like a place where deals were closed and promotions were celebrated. The Thiel Foundation had arranged for winners and their parents to meet one another over lunch as they decided whether or not to take the offers. Now that their children had been awarded spots in the program, some parents had concerns about their children moving alone to the West Coast, incorporating companies, and finding their own housing.

The Thiel Foundation couldn't house them but would provide them with weekly social activities, lunches, and lectures, as well as assistance with financial logistics. James O'Neill, head of the Thiel Foundation and a managing director of Clarium Capital, and his team would organize orientation retreats and seminars.

A tall, lanky guy in his early forties, O'Neill had a style that was scholar-geek, featuring wacky bow ties atop two shirts with collars. At night, he often donned a red velvet blazer to dinner parties. That day, he introduced himself and said that he and his then wife lived in Marin County, where they homeschooled their three children.

John Burnham's parents, Stephen and Krysia Burnham, approved of this idea, and said they taught their son more out of school than he learned in it. After Stephen graduated from Dartmouth and Krysia from Smith College, the two met in New York, where Stephen was a stockbroker and Krysia was an assistant at *Elle* magazine. They now lived in Newton, Massachusetts, and had flown in that morning for the lunch. They beamed as they introduced themselves to finalist David Merfield's father. He had just arrived from Singapore.

"John has always acted out in school," Stephen boasted, adding with a laugh, "He may as well pull up a chair outside the principal's office." Stephen found his son's rebelliousness to be a sign of creativity and further proof that the fellowship suited him. "School just isn't for John," his father said. "He's four years ahead of the other kids."

The Burnhams explained how they now thought of the Thiel

Fellowship as a new kind of status symbol. It said their son could get into Harvard but turned it down for something better—even though he didn't. That he was a fellow was yet another reason why his opting out of the typical path explained all those years of acting out. Now, sanctioned by a Silicon Valley success story, John was on a new track, one that his parents hoped might be more compelling than college.

The other parents nodded knowingly before Jim O'Neill motioned for everyone to take their seats around the long dining table.

At one end were John Marbach and Sherry Pressler, finalist Jonathan Marbach's parents, and Praveen and Tanu Tyle, parents of Sujay Tyle, another finalist. Marbach was the closest a fellow would come to looking like a jock. A tall, athletic high school senior with light-brown hair, big, round eyes, and a ski jump nose, he looked like a ladies' man. More sociable and talkative than the rest, it mattered to him if someone liked him or not. The others acted as if they didn't care. John Jr. asked questions and listened intently. He made friends easily among the other potential fellows.

"It's funny," said Marbach's mother, Sherry, "but as parents, it's very strange that this is happening, because we saved all our lives for Jonathan to go to college, and now he's not." She paused. "But it seems like just getting in gives you enough status, so it's like getting the Thiel Fellowship is better than actually going to college." She said it in a wistful way, as if she hadn't quite accepted the idea of one of her children getting into college and then deciding against it.

"Yeah, it's like you're above Harvard because you don't have to go," said her husband. "We always put aside money for this, forever, and here the day comes, and he's not using it!" he added. They laughed. "Maybe we should just travel!"

After the parents and students around the table introduced themselves, their children waved at one another shyly. O'Neill stood up to make an announcement.

"Peter's theory is that for the past fifty years, all of us have gotten accustomed to steady economic growth and a constant stream of innovation and productivity, and that innovation rudder has slowed down and so has economic growth," O'Neill said. "He's very worried that innovation is lagging and is trying to do everything he can to increase the rate of innovation."

On the for-profit side, O'Neill explained, Thiel will invest in companies that fulfill this mandate, and, on the nonprofit side, in bright young innovators—hence the birth of the Thiel Fellowship. "He's had some great experiences in tech investing for young people," O'Neill added, mentioning William and Michael Andregg, two brothers who'd dropped out of college to start Halcyon Molecular. Although now defunct, their genome scanning company was once valued at close to $100 million. "And he had a kid come to him one time to invest in a social networking company called Facebook," he said, laughing, "and he invested in that."

Since many of the finalists worried that once they became fellows, they would want to change their ideas, O'Neill tried to put them at ease by describing how Thiel and his cofounders drastically changed the idea for PayPal before it launched. At first, Thiel wanted PayPal to beam payments through Palm Pilots, with email as a feature. One of his cofounders, Elon Musk, had started the competing X.com, which was a financial services company with email payments as only a feature. The two eventually joined forces to start what is now PayPal by making the secondary feature the main idea.

On a plane ride to San Francisco, when O'Neill, Thiel, and Luke Nosek were talking about the need for innovation, they first thought of having a group of twenty-five-year-olds propose ideas for them to invest in. But then they realized by the time most people are twenty-five, many are burdened by student debt or locked into tracked careers. Plus, they thought that talented people in their midtwenties would already have social access to investors.

"But what the world economy needs is people at the right stage of life able to take a little financial risk to help them get started," explained O'Neill. "So we devised the fellowship for people under twenty, called 'Twenty Under Twenty,' a good, manageable number." The foundation would be there to help them hire employees and find investors, as well as advise them on their business plans. "This is the time to be very frank," he said. "We're already committed to you. We don't have a stake in this financially, but we do have a stake in making it succeed." He made a final clarification: "You know you have to stop out, not drop out," he reassured them. "In two years, you can always go back to school." He ended with a different option: "Lots of people start companies and leave school and never want to go back, and that's fine, and others do."

O'Neill said the goal was for fellows to start companies, nonprofits, or tech projects, but they could find mentors at existing companies. Thiel and the Founders Fund wouldn't have equity in any of the fellows' companies, but technically they could be recruited to work at Thiel's companies. But he encouraged them all to head to Palo Alto, where Thiel and the other founders lived most of the time.

Some of the finalists wanted to enroll in college for just the fall semester, so that they had the option to return if they wanted to later. Finalist Marbach would be attending Wake Forest University to test out his education start-up that would provide students with online classes and virtual teachers with actual teachers and students, though his cofounders would be starting immediately. He wished he would too. Eager to drop out of school at the end of the year, they thought Marbach was noncommittal, and worried that once he did leave, he might not be able to catch up.

Marbach's family had just flown in from North Carolina, where they had been visiting Wake Forest the day before. After spending $600 per person on airfare alone, his father seemed relieved not to have to pay for more than the semester.

"People spend two hundred thousand dollars on college; then after graduation in May or June, everyone moves back in with their parents," said John Marbach. "Empty nesters get the birds back in the nest."

About half of the families were immigrants. The Tyles, originally from India, were dressed formally, she in a conservative dress with muted colors and he in a dark suit. They'd moved to America for its educational opportunities. Tanu enrolled in a master's program in architecture at Washington University, and Praveen earned a PhD in pharmaceutics. But over the years, she had become disillusioned with both American parenting and education.

"In India, people are street-smart," she said. "Here they grow up with the positive reinforcement and all this seclusion, so they end up really innocent and naïve." There is "misuse of education" in India too, she conceded, but there at least, "it's cheap, so it doesn't matter. Here it is a risk."

Tanu felt that American children never get to know what real life is like until their education ends. "Before going to college, it should always be a prerequisite to have life experience," she said. She found Americans' tracked educations and careers linear, but lacking purpose and direction. For her, the Thiel Fellowship solved that problem. "Doing things like this requires courage," she said. "Thiel has been supporting that, and forcing kids to break away from those bonds."

Tanu said she wished her older son, Sheel, had applied. Instead, he was still enrolled at Stanford, though he worked three days a week meeting with new companies at Bessemer Venture Partners, a Silicon Valley venture capital firm. "I said to him, 'You should see this excitement and energy!'"

Her other son, finalist Sujay, had been doing ethanol research with a professor at the University of Rochester, in upstate New York, since he was eight years old. "Even the professor was giving up, but Sujay persisted and persisted," said Tanu.

Professors and deans around the country didn't seem to agree. In 2011 Vivek Wadhwa, a visiting scholar at Duke and Emory Universities, wrote a column for TechCrunch called "Friends Don't Let Friends Take Education Advice from Peter Thiel," in which he bashed the fellowship. During a conference panel discussion at the American Society for Engineering Education Engineering Deans Institute, Wadhwa had raised the topic of Peter Thiel's views on education. As he wrote, "Most of the deans in the audience were aghast. They couldn't believe that there were debates like this happening in Silicon Valley. I told them that more than a dozen students had approached me over the past few months asking for advice on whether they should drop out; that students took people like Thiel very seriously." Wadhwa interviewed three of the deans in attendance. One of them, Jim Plummer of Stanford's School of Engineering, compared Thiel's idea to that of college athletes taking no academic classes and instead just playing their sport until they are drafted. Duke University Pratt School of Engineering dean Tom Katsouleas said, "The other reason one should not take Peter Thiel's advice is that the value of education is intrinsic and an end in itself rather than something to be measured by its career financial return."

Ironically, Thiel himself had undergraduate and graduate degrees from Stanford. He was used to questions about that contradiction. He said that college made sense for some people—such as for him—but for most, it didn't. He said he wouldn't have changed anything, but if he'd had a great idea back then, he would have gone for it.

Parents at the luncheon found the deans' complaints to be cheap shots, considering that their entire identities were tied up in academia. They went back to discussing the Harvard Business School professor who had approved of the fellowship. They said that while she wasn't entirely in favor of the idea, she was open to accepting someone who had tried the fellowship and then returned to school.

"She is supportive, and that's the whole point," said Tanu. Still, John Marbach imagined that his other children would have more tracked paths. John Jr. was one of triplets. His sister Megan was going to Fairfield University for nursing in the fall, while his sister Melanie would be attending Loyola University Maryland. As if paying one college tuition bill wasn't enough, the Marbachs were faced with three all at the same time.

In the end, only one finalist awarded a fellowship that year turned it down. Tessa Green, an eighteen-year-old high school senior from Westport, Connecticut, had been vacillating between accepting the award and going to MIT, where her parents thought she should go. O'Neill took her to lunch later that week in New York. To help convince Tessa, he invited along Eden Full, a gung-ho finalist who had built a solar-powered "sun saluter" for Kenyan villages as her project. The two girls had roomed together at the Hyatt.

But when Green showed up at Fig & Olive on Fifty-Second Street and Madison Avenue in Manhattan on her way to a pre-frosh weekend at Princeton, where she had also been accepted, she was apprehensive to even begin the discussion. With her wavy brown hair splayed in every direction on top of her head until it reached back into a ponytail, she hoisted her heavy backpack off her shoulder and pushed her glasses up onto her nose. She had just spent the past two weeks arguing with her parents about taking the fellowship versus going to school, and everything they had said had pushed her in a college-bound direction. It did not help that her father, a corporate lawyer, had bombarded her with questions about how she planned to start a company, where she would live, and how she would find funding.

In the past few days, she had found out about her fellowship offer as well as her acceptances to both MIT and Princeton. It seemed like all she wanted to do was get on the train to be in the safe confines of a college campus and back to what she thought she was supposed to be doing.

"Would it help if I called your parents and talked to them about the details?" O'Neill asked.

"Yes, but I don't know what they'll say," the teenager said hesitantly. "Maybe they would feel better to know the program will be supervised?" she offered, though it seemed she just wanted him to stop trying to persuade her. She would have to make her decision within the next week, and despite the entire Facebook chat group of finalists trying to convince her to take it, Tessa declined.

Burnham, however, practically had his bags packed. He'd endured a dismal spring semester after breaking his arm over the winter, which prevented him from playing any sports. The wrestling team was pretty much the only part of school he enjoyed. None of his friends was surprised that he'd taken the fellowship. "People were really supportive," he said. John left high school early, deciding he would take his remaining classes remotely from Palo Alto until graduation.

Meanwhile, farther south along the row of ship terminals at

the Port of Miami, house music was blaring from a cruise gate at the end of North Cruise Drive. Out front, an army of young men and women in fluorescent green uniforms was beckoning new arrivals toward the beat of the bass. The sound was coming from Terminal D, where the welcome staff was pointing passengers up an escalator to a veritable techno rave. There in the cavernous embarkation area, a snaking line longer than John F. Kennedy International Airport's on Christmas Eve inched along so slowly that the rhythm of the music felt even faster, throwing the crowd into desperate anticipation. Dressed in fedoras, nautical striped cotton shirts, and frilly neon sundresses, the young group stood on line at least two hours before they reached the counters up front.

They were not auditioning for a reality show, but attending Summit at Sea, an annual Summit Series conference that had grown from nineteen boys in a ski house to an eight-hundred-person extravaganza in DC to a whole resort and living community in Eden, Utah, attracting speakers like Bill Clinton and Ted Turner. Its current incarnation consisted of a thousand hand-picked entrepreneurs and celebrities aboard a Celebrity Century cruise ship about to head to the Bahamas from the Port of Miami. Among them were Zappos CEO Tony Hsieh, hip-hop impresario Russell Simmons, former first daughter Barbara Bush, and actress Kristen Bell. Virgin Group founder Richard Branson was already on the boat and scheduled to give an opening speech that afternoon. Thiel would arrive that night. The event was the brainchild of five hipsters in their midtwenties who were constantly clad in form-fitting T-shirts, thigh-hugging jeans, and nouveau high-tops with the tongues sticking out. They sported unruly hairstyles with varying spikes and curls.

It was the first day of what would be a three-day floating networking party and one of the first meetings of some members of Thiel's new 20 Under 20 team. The fellows had been chosen and now their decision to ditch the institution of college deserved some real attention. Patri Friedman was in attendance as research for his Seasteading "cruise," but was spending most of the trip figuring out how to bring the Thiel fellows out west—in the most dramatic fashion. He walked around the deck shirtless, or wearing a flowing purple cape and a paper crown from Burger King.

But aside from Friedman and his fellow geeks from Silicon Valley, the ship was filled mostly with men who had taken metrosexuality to the gym. Though only forming one-fourth of the crowd, the women onboard looked West Coast casual in cotton dresses and loose, sheer T-shirts bearing East Coast labels. Disciples of attendee Tim Ferriss, the author of *The 4-Hour Workweek* and, most recently, *The 4-Hour Body*, both boys and girls were there to hypernetwork with millionaire company founders—and they wanted to look good doing it. Dubbed the Davos of the younger generation, Summit Series actually exemplified much more. Its founders, DC-born Justin Cohen, Elliott Bisnow, and Jeff Rosenthal, had unearthed a new social code, almost an entirely new generational personality, in which hundreds of twenty- and thirty-somethings would be walking around a cruise ship unabashedly wearing Bluetooth "poken" necklaces, plastic white pendants shaped like cartoon hands with Bluetooth technology programmed with the user's contact. Instead of exchanging business cards, wearers could simply touch necklaces together to exchange each other's information and later plug the necklace into their computer's USB port. There, they could log in to the ship's own private social network called "The Collective" and download the contact information of anyone they met during their scheduled bonding activities, such as "speed-networking," poker lessons, and life coaching sessions on deck or at the cruise's lone stop on "Imagine Nation" island. Imagine Nation, more officially known as Coco Cay, is a man-made island with ice cream stands, water slides, folding lounge chairs, kayaks, ropes courses, and beach volleyball, all built specifically for passing cruise ships. En route, the Summit at Sea participants would wake up for "mandatory team building exercises," otherwise known as fire drills, take meditation guided by the Venerable Lama Tenzin Dhonden, attend lectures by successful tech entrepreneurs such as Thiel, and party with Swedish DJ Axwell, English musician Imogen Heap, and hip-hop band The Roots.

By boarding the ship, all one thousand of them had Arrived, and gone was the snobbery-meets-sprezzatura attitude of the formerly cool.

The cruisers were nouveau-nerdy, a cross between the Williamsburg hipster, the navel-gazing Tim Ferriss–following autosexual, and of course its predecessor, the metrosexual. During lectures, aisles were filled with entrepreneurs jumping from row to row to give elevator pitches to anyone sitting alone. "Where are you from?" they asked, before launching into their company's founding and description. They capped off the mini meeting with a kiss of the Bluetooth necklace they held up to meet yours. Then they linked to their newfound friends on The Collective, which turned out to be a Facebook-meets-Match.com for cruisers.

Peter Thiel's talk was the most anticipated, and Friedman had a front row seat where he sat cross-legged in his purple board shorts, white tank top, and pirate hat, grinning.

Over the course of the cruise he'd made progress in his and Thiel's plan to pick up the fellows on a bus and drive them across the country. Deliberately modeled on the bus trip Ken Kesey and his band of Merry Pranksters took from near Palo Alto to New York in 1964, Thiel and his partners were planning a bus trip in the opposite direction. Kesey had exhorted the youth of America to "move off dead center" (in much the same way that Timothy Leary would later advise young people to "turn on, tune in, drop out") into a lotus land of LSD, psilocybin, hashish, and locoweed in order to "open the doors of perception" (in Aldous Huxley's phrase). Thiel's idea was that the bus trip would exhort American youth to "stop out," drop out of the comatose

American education system and get smart, turn on their powers of invention, tune in to billions of dollars before age thirty—ideally before age twenty—and renew America's position as the world center of innovation.

Friedman and his friend James Hogan, the founder of Ephemerisle, a yearly gathering of ramshackle boats tied together as a floating precursor to actual Seasteading, were its appointed leaders, and here on this ship, Friedman had come up with a budget.

"Come on, I'll show you!" he said, and bounded down the ship's central spiral staircase to a cabin he was sharing with two roommates. Next to a stack of new flyers for the Seasteading Institute, Friedman opened his laptop to a spreadsheet listing a monthlong schedule of rallies, concerts, and lecture events from Harvard to Yale across the country to Stanford. There were two versions, one labeled "epic." The budget: $1.7 million.

Thiel's team—Friedman, Hogan, and a few Founders Fund employees—wanted this bus to be a far cry from the school bus the Merry Pranksters drove from California to the East Coast to spread their psychedelic cult, encouraging followers to embrace their inner wild child, "be what you are and don't apologize for it"—whether it be frolicking in swamps or rolling naked down the side of the road. This new bus would have a specific purpose and direction. Whereas the Merry Pranksters' journey across the country was a "superprank" ending in New York to shock the pants off the squares, the end goal of the new tour was to put brilliant brains to work.

Instead of all-inclusive, the vibe would be exclusive, its style high-tech and sleek, not retro-fluorescent. The tour would commence at Harvard, the very bastion of the breed of East Coast elitism they found so ineffectual. Famous college "stop outs" such as Facebook's Dustin Moskowitz would give talks at campuses across the country to persuade kids to follow through on whatever crazy idea they thought of in the freshman dining hall rather than bury it under a risk-averse, self-esteem-laden curriculum. The trip would be a countrywide call to reject the lax, coddling environment plaguing America's higher education system—created in part by Kesey's own intellectual disciples.

But fast-forward a few months, and the bus trip fell apart. The Founders Fund partners who were at first game to participate soon realized they didn't really want to spend an entire month on a bus with twenty teenagers, especially when they had plenty of work to do at home. In fall 2011 they scrapped the plan, and the fellows started trickling in to Palo Alto one by one.

2

The Gluten-Free Open Marriage

John Burnham had never been to a polyamorous community. Growing up on the East Coast, he always thought that sort of thing wasn't only "not done," it wasn't even talked about. He'd just arrived in the Bay Area over the summer of 2011, and had few friends and little social contact. But he started hearing about the somewhat unusual social lives of people in his new circle, such as his mentor Patri Friedman.

Burnham was renting a pool house in Atherton, which was about a half-hour walk from anything resembling a store. Few of the other Thiel fellows lived nearby. The ones that did stuck to themselves. Burnham missed having people to talk to. He called Danielle Strachman, who organized social activities for the fellows.

She and her boyfriend lived with Friedman at a housing complex its occupants had named Tortuga, a few miles south in Mountain View. At the time, Friedman subscribed to a polyamorous lifestyle, as did most of the other eight people living in the two combined houses that comprised Tortuga. Strachman and Hogan were monogamous, but Friedman had a coparent, and they had two children. But the coparent was also in a relationship with one of their roommates, and Patri had a relationship—albeit casual—with the roommate's girlfriend on some nights. All of them were free to do as they pleased. They could swap rooms, people, houses, and then end up back with their "primaries."

The lifestyle surprised Burnham, and he was opposed to it morally. "It's not like I was up in arms about it; my general feeling was (and still is) that it's not really any of my business," he recalls. He was mostly perplexed at how anyone in the valley could find one viable female to mate with, let alone many. His fellowship class was mostly male, and while nearly every fellow had a crush on Laura Deming, none of them had succeeded in wooing her.

Some people who didn't do well in school headed out to Silicon Valley because they wanted to be let off the leash to do something innovative, and out here, that feeling tended to spill over into sexuality. Those who had been unlucky in love back home found hope here. They found friends willing to be just as experimental in the bedroom as they were in the lab. Those who maybe didn't make it on the football field or the cheerleading squad were now in a place where it was encouraged to unwind and "get weird."

Polyamory intrigued Burnham, though he didn't subscribe to it. Friedman did too. Granted, he wasn't as excited about Friedman's Seasteading Institute. When he saw what Seasteading actually was, he remembered thinking, "I was a little underwhelmed." Designs for it involved a concrete platform with makeshift metal shelters sitting way out in the ocean.

Living on the East Coast, Burnham had come from a family of sailors. "One of the characteristics in my family is this love of the ocean and sleeping on a boat, setting sail; that's part of the poetry of the Burnham family," he said wistfully. "One of the things that deeply disappointed me about Seasteading is I didn't get the sense of the sea." Seasteading's proposed aquatic communities would be close enough to land to commute but far enough to escape government control. They had none of the majesty and sense of freedom of a sailboat, he thought.

Burnham had a grander vision of freedom. Polyamory was nothing like what he imagined to be Hugh Hefner's Playboy grotto. But still, Friedman had long been a hero of Burnham's, and he was interested to see what this new life was all about.

Although, at five foot four and 111 pounds, Friedman wasn't the typical ladies' man, he had a good time flirting with fellow techies, whom he wooed with his wit and his rather uncaring disrespect for authority—apparent currency, sexually and other-wise, in Silicon Valley. Lately Friedman had been having diffi-culty with his wife, who was now spending more time with his roommate than with him. "I have needs too!" he'd exclaim. But his wife didn't want to break off anything with their roommate, nor meet Patri's "needs," as he requested.

On some mornings Friedman and his roommates would go to Hobee's diner in Sunnyvale. There a group of techie couples in their late twenties and early thirties filed in for breakfast. They would order pollo supremo tacos and chicken apple sau-sage scrambles off a special gluten-free menu and then talk about libertarian ideas, such as holding events in ponds and lakes with rafts that might prepare them for their eventual free-floating is-land communities in the middle of the ocean.

Other mornings, they might come in and do it again—but possibly with different partners. Some in the group had made a choice to be "poly," or have one "primary" mate, with the option for others. They blogged about it, of course. They called it con-scious living.

Tortuga was the brainchild of Friedman, but Strachman, her boyfriend, and nearly a dozen other Bay Area techies lived there too. The ex-wife's new boyfriend, the roommate, a "rationalist," and his primary girlfriend also lived there. The girlfriend worked as a college testing tutor.

Along with cohousing and sharing partners, many of the group members were hyperaware of their diets. They had tried the carb-free, meat-heavy Paleo diet, as well as intermittent fasting. Being gluten free was a given. In a post about his new yoga class, Friedman wrote, "Regular acrobatic activity is a key part of my self-care," a not unusual topic on his once prolific, now defunct blog *patrissimo*. Friedman settled on a version of the Paleo diet in which he carried around sticks of butter and coconut oil to add to his meals at restaurants, so he would fill up with less food.

He and his ex-wife had been "polyamorous" for more than ten years. In this arrangement, they had been married for six. Their Facebook profile pages said "in an open relationship." The past summer, Friedman first bristled at his wife's dating their roommate, so he moved out. But then the ex-wife missed him, and so the two started a trial separation. "I told her I wanted another family later in life, so I think she was always worried she wouldn't be my primary forever," he lamented. "There were times I felt bad, like, 'poly should be easier than this—we're an embarrassment,' but several friends said, 'Are you kidding? You guys are amazing!'" he wrote on his blog. Friends wrote in to comment, mentioning the typical patterns they saw: "Guy and girl in serious relationship decide to have an open relationship—Guy dates various girls on the side over time, girl doesn't happen to have any outside opportunities but is fine with this. Girl finally meets one outside guy, who she starts dating—Guy flips a shit, everything explodes."

Experimental behavior wasn't limited to the valley, of course. In May 2014, a group of mostly middle-aged men was filing into an empty, steamy warehouse deep in the Mission District (aka the Mission), a formerly undesirable neighborhood of San Francisco that was now home to a host of tech companies. Some were also in open relationships and participated in polyamorous groups such as OneTaste, in which women sit around in a circle to be sexually aroused by anonymous paying customers under the guise of both therapy and a newfangled philosophical sexual awakening.

The dinner was a "Death Over Dinner." It was spearheaded by a former-chef-turned-open-relationship proponent named Michael Hebb. After he disrupted monogamy, he planned to "transgress" death. This disruption was going to happen by talking about it at a series of dinners he had launched with the science journalist David Ewing Duncan. Frustrated by the lack of paying prospects in the media world, Duncan had just started an events-planning business called Arc Programs, in which he would host panels on artificial intelligence and humans becoming more machinelike.

Inside the dark, cavernous space, the tables were set up in

an X (for the chromosome, of course), although out of fifty attendees, only three of them had two X chromosomes. While
death and longevity were the focus of the evening, the dinner
was only foreplay before the after party, where traditional sexual
roles would be rejected. To get warmed up for this "disruptive
transgression," guests received cards listing options of a, b, c, and
d, in order of escalating willingness to upload their minds and
bodies into a chip and take the artificial intelligence plunge. (The
idea was that in the future it might be possible to develop a chip
or nanobot onto which one could copy all the information in the
brain.) Duncan and Hebb announced that the evening's seating
would be based on how everyone filled out those cards, making
it clear that the more of oneself you uploaded, the more of your
body you would entrust to artificial intelligence, and the braver,
more enlightened you were.

Ironically, while man as machine was being glorified up
onstage, the audience was served the most organic, artisanal,
straight-from-a-dirt-patch cuisine ever seen. Passed around in
earthen bowls were what looked like blobs of soil and mush. Each
vegan mushball had the gravelly taste of not animal, vegetable,
or mineral, but of sediment. As the starved men looked around,
pushing the blobs back and forth on their plates, they went for
the wine instead, which if artisanal and organic was at least still
alcoholic. Ravenous, they were ready for the rest of the evening,
which entailed a long walk across an empty parking lot in front

of a Walmart lot toward a row of abandoned buildings next to a highway underpass.

But that was still a good half hour away. When dinner finished, Reese Jones, one of the founders of Singularity University, sat in the center of a circle of admirers in the front of the room, expounding upon the philosophy of OneTaste, the "orgasmic community" Jones helped support. He explained how women sat around in a circle cross-legged, naked from the waist down, and men sat behind them, caressing them until they orgasmed but without having an orgasm themselves. Wearing pressed khakis and a white button-down shirt, Jones, with greying bushy hair and a grey beard, looked more like a disheveled professor than a sexual innovator. But as he described how this practice was not only disruptive but also enlightening, his face took on a fervor of a lusty teenager. His friends sitting nearby, a mix of other venture capitalists, Singularity University professors, and Thiel fellow mentors, were in agreement. They all wanted to achieve a new level of freedom. They thought that this new liberated sexuality would bring them to a new level of enlightenment. Some of them said they liked visiting the Russian baths north of San Francisco where they could bathe en masse in the nude and feel "fully alive."

What Silicon Valley could do for social mores, where hierarchies didn't matter, and nor did family names or Ivy Leagues, it could do for sex. In the start-up world, making a wild, bold, bad decision—even if it resulted in catastrophic failure—was a resume builder.

Could Silicon Valley hack ethics too? Religion in Silicon Valley was really a formalized hobby. Yoga in Silicon Valley was no longer yoga. Engineers recoded yoga to be a "religious, meditative, transformative, disruptive, transgressive" experience. Yogic gurus with nearly the level of Tony Robbins led these new religious belief systems. Yoga instructors were body engineers. Flexibility coders. Mind leaders. The guru would not only sweep in and out of your Sunday morning, but he would also take you on vacation retreats or spice up your marriage. It was not exercise, it was life choreography, spirituality, and psychiatry all rolled into one.

That evening, the after party would take place in an unkempt, practically abandoned building like Huffman's converted garages, which had become work spaces by day and raves by night. Molecular biologist and Thiel fellow mentor Todd Huffman and his wife, Katy, had been working on creating a better, faster way to see images on a microscope. They worked with various fellows on their biology projects and welcomed them into their unorthodox fold.

Both had pink hair and wore matching outfits: usually grey T-shirts and black pants. Huffman said that the occupants of Langton Labs were on a spectrum from fully monogamous to fully polyamorous. "San Franciscans have words for relationships the way that Eskimos have words for snow," he joked. "Langton Labs is a good cross section of the community." During the weekdays, they worked in the basement of a community that Huffman founded called Langton Laboratories. But what they ended up creating turned out to be much more. Langton Labs was an alternative institution that served as part living space with sixteen bedrooms with mattresses, crammed chockablock into nooks and crannies of an old row house on Langton Street in the Mission, and part all-year stage design studio for Burning Man.

Burning Man is a thirty-year-old festival in the middle of the Nevada Desert that had gone from being a small, cultish campground for alternative artists to a sprawling experimental playground for anyone who wanted to feel like they fit in while in what they considered their "rawest" state. That could entail painting their naked bodies in a shimmery gold tint, wearing furry horns, and riding around on a bike covered in fluorescent streamers. In recent years, Silicon Valley had gravitated to the festival, especially for its symbolic breaking of social codes.

Here at Langton Labs, Huffman hoped to extend that feeling. He and Katy weren't outwardly after money. Their aspirations were larger: they wanted to hack living. Down the street was their work space, where other start-ups' machinery overflowed off every counter and desktop and shelf. Those were just the core group who worked here. The community that revolved around the space could be as many as three hundred people. Huffman didn't know. He said he would accept anyone who wanted to "break [his] own boundaries."

For most young people in Silicon Valley—comprised disproportionately of men—breaking boundaries meant drumming up the courage even to speak to a romantic interest. It was a place many young men thought of as a "technical wasteland," where eligible women were few and far between. Like going to college, here nerds were suddenly placed in a new world with no adult supervision, where transgressing at work was encouraged as much as transgressing in life. Granted, not everyone in Silicon Valley was polyamorous, not all couples had open marriages, but those that did felt more than comfortable crowing about it. It was like the gluten-free joke "How do you know if someone's gluten-free?" Answer: "They tell you."

Fetching Laura Deming was always being recruited for these kinds of activities. People were always trying to "open her eyes" to new ways of thinking and living. She was a Silicon Valley geek's dream.

The valley was different from San Francisco, of course. Down in Palo Alto, men far outnumbered women. Those stuck there would often couple up as soon as they could, like bears finding mates for the long, cold winter. Coding all day left little time to play, plus bars in Palo Alto tended to close around ten. Those looking for excitement (or a date on the fly) would head into the city—mostly to the Mission. All sorts of experimentation was available there.

Burnham, at first stuck down in suburban Atherton, where most women in his neighborhood were married and in their mid-forties, relished these trips into the city. By late April 2014, any party was a good party. Even if Todd Huffman's style wasn't necessarily his—no one at sailing camp on the East Coast would dare wear his hair with a pink curl in front or wear such a dull black-and-grey outfit.

They also wouldn't plant sensors under their skin to alert cryogenics facilities if anything were to happen to them. Huffman, on the other hand, had not only sensors in his body but also instructions tattooed on his torso explaining how he should be frozen in a thermos at Alcor Life Extension Foundation, the cryonics organization, should he expire.

Huffman, thirty-seven, grew up in Long Beach. He was an early participant in Langton Labs when it started seven years ago. He moved in six years ago and was on the lease for one of its two warehouses. He added the lab building down the street a few years later and made money by charging rent to the dozens of people living and working there. Sixteen people lived in the housing section, off open living rooms through corridors and over Burning Man dance floors and bike space.

The morning after one of their famed parties, they were sitting downstairs in their lab testing their new microscope.

Research labs at universities sent the Huffmans tissue for them to image and process the data. They said their machines could image the tissue hundreds of times faster than a human could, and do as much imaging in one day as a human technician could in a whole year.

The ways that technology could revolutionize science had Huffman fired up—and also pointed to the possibilities of machines outrunning us, he thought. It made him wonder why we were sticking to our own petty human rules, if so much more was possible. Wasn't there something more? he wondered. Here he could prove there was.

Huffman said that three of his live-in entrepreneurs were dropouts of PhD programs. "No full-time or founding team have completed a PhD," he said. "To me there needs to be the world after academics, but academics is a paved road, and then it stops."

Where that road stopped, the path to San Francisco started. Here there was a level of energy and tolerance for risk that had so far been unparalleled in other places. "You can find lots of smart places like any of the national labs at universities. They have the depth of knowledge, but they don't have the tolerance for risk, and they don't have the fiercely independent traditions," said Huffman. Here it was these traditions that had defined the new set of people who pursued experimental living with religious intensity. With a group that knew no bounds, these pseudo orgies, raves, and newfangled salons created a bizarre, warped version of regular life, with a wider lens on normality. Here institutions and routines such as raises, rents, mortgages—marriage—were as inconsequential, breakable, and flexible as the industries technology disrupted.

Huffman saw his purpose as far higher than mere style or culture. He thought of his role as creating a new zeitgeist for an adventurous Silicon Valley demographic. "There's such a high density of intelligent, well-educated people here," he said. "This zip code has the highest level of education in the world." Because of this, he believed that anything was possible technologically. He pointed across the street to a nondescript glass door in an old warehouse, where a couple was leaning against the wall sipping lattes. "Right over there—they're building satellites," he said. "They've launched twenty-eight satellites."

He conceded that there were places outside of Silicon Valley that were trying to do the same thing, but they didn't have the same interactivity. At the MIT Media Lab or the Harvard Innovation Lab, people weren't sleeping on the floor next to their microscopes. They weren't partying in the hallways in between teacher conference rooms. There was not as much autonomy—and far too much bureaucracy at any of these "legacy institutions," aka universities.

There, according to Huffman, people couldn't switch frames as easily—or beds, for that matter. Talents were more siloed. Here social life reflected work through creativity and trial and error. While his roommates built robots that assemble electronics, created circuit boards, and empowered machines, they were becoming what he considered "fully alive."

In his estimation, the entire East Coast was stuck in a zombie state, and the young fellows he mentored, such as Burnham, Deming, and Proud, could make it in Silicon Valley if they only let go of the structures they used to know.

Meanwhile, Burnham's old mentor, Patri Friedman, was having more and more trouble in his experimental community. His wife had asked for a trial separation. Friedman wasn't sure what that meant for both his family and his belief in polyamory. He wasn't happy about it.

3

Hippy-Dippy Coding Communes

By the end of the summer of 2011, John Burnham was start-ing to realize he had to give up on mining for asteroids, at least for now. He was disheartened to realize that the founder of the XPrize Foundation, Peter Diamandis, had already started working on it years before, with far more capital and expertise. John was also getting lonely down in Atherton. Aside from Patri Friedman and occasionally some of the fellows, he never really saw anyone he knew.

He went to a few other Thiel events where he met more po-tential mentors: some during Friday lunches in Palo Alto, and others on retreats by the Thiel Foundation organizers. "Some of them I got along with really well—some people really like me, some just can't stand me, some people really dislike me, and I just have to accept that," he remembers thinking. Mostly, though, his social life was disheartening.

He was worried that Diamandis and his asteroid mining company would eclipse any effort he made. "They actually have a decent chance of getting it done," he admitted. "I've been doing planetary mining research since I was sixteen, but they have the capital." So instead, Burnham dropped the idea and started interning at Moon Express, a company dedicated to researching how to mine minerals on the moon. There he worked in business development, mostly typing up marketing materials. After a few months, he left to intern at Cosmogia (now called Planet Labs), another space industry firm that he refused to talk about. "I have an NDA"—a nondisclosure agreement—he explained.

That job didn't last long, as it didn't take much for Burnham to realize that working in an office as part of a staff was not for him. "I put on a pretty good show of being an extrovert," he said, "but I can't learn with people in the same room." Conventional employment simply wouldn't work for him. "I end up staying up all night and doing all the work, then going into the office and being like, 'Well, what do I do now?'" he said. "I had a wonderful experience, but I'm just a crappy employee."

So Burnham decided he should try out one of the new

co-living spaces he had heard about. It wouldn't be quite so lonely, and maybe it wouldn't be a bad place to find his next big idea. It was a new way of living that harkened back to the hippy days of the 1960s, when some young people lived together in communes. But the big difference was that these weren't places for kicking back and tuning out. In today's co-living communities, people worked hard, often all night. Coding and programming into the wee hours almost came with the rent.

In Silicon Valley, working together and playing together wasn't just a college motto. The twenty- and thirty-year-old inhabitants had taken dorm culture and amped it up further than they ever could on campus.

Instead of the earlier progression of going to college to live among students, then leaving campus for a big city with a roommate or two, and finally living on one's own, in the Bay Area, that pattern often went backward. Instead of the adult trajectory in which each new dwelling increasingly resembles the life of an adult human with a career and a family, Silicon Valley's housing steps went the opposite way, where the more advanced and enlightened you were, the crazier your idea, the more "disruptive" a living situation you could find.

In the late aughts, these selective housing units started springing up through the valley. Much like that first Hewlett-Packard garage spawned thousands of other companies started in garages, the movie *The Social Network*'s depiction of a co-living house, where dozens of nerdy engineers worked on building Facebook until Justin Timberlake, as Sean Parker, turned their coding session into a rager, co-living communities had taken hold. The object of these wasn't for roommates to live among their kind or for other grown-ups to partake in shared responsibilities. It was still a way to save money, but to do so in a techie-chic way. Just as there was no shame over working in a garage if you're building the next Google, there was no shame in sleeping on a shelf in a pool house if you have a wacky start-up vision to balance out your lack of bedroom.

Two other fellows in Burnham's class, Alex Kiselev and Jeffrey Lim, were living with a half dozen other local entrepreneurs in a co-living mansion in San Francisco they had named the Glint (spelled TheGlint). Alex was working on developing an open-source spectrometer, a tool used to measure spectra, while Jeffrey tried a number of start-up ideas but ended up working as a software developer at Ripple Labs. Thanks to TheGlint, Burnham now had ample opportunity to meet the right people. In the evenings, it would host area venture capitalists to speak and have dinner, such as Bing Gordon of KPCB; Senem Diyici and the Mavi Yol Quartet "for a night of music and experimentation"; and Cynthia Ong, founder of LEAP (Land Empowerment Animals People), for a "flash fund-raising event" aimed at empowering the people of Sarawak, a Malaysian state on the island of Borneo, that had become, according to the housemates, victim of "heavy timber exploitation followed by massive grabbing of Native Customary Right land for oil palm plantations."

TheGlint had even loftier aspirations. Kiselev and a few friends rented the space to make it part home, part ideas salon. They called it a "hero accelerator." *Heroism* had become another buzzword in Silicon Valley—almost as popular as *disrupt* and *transgress* and *super fun*. It was even the name of a new university started down in Palo Alto by venture capitalist Tim Draper. At Draper University, students lived in dorms called "Hero City," where instead of learning English and math, they took classes called "Vision & Future" and "Special Powers." A year later, Draper would be among the unfortunate investors who'd put money into Theranos, Elizabeth Holmes's company whose much-ballyhooed blood testing machine was later found not to work as claimed.

At TheGlint, the fellows worked on their own but still lived together. Since the beginning of the fellowship, Kiselev had been toiling on an "inexpensive high-performance liquid chromatography system," a tool to make it easier for scientists to analyze lab samples. Over the past year, he and a number of other Thiel fellows had lived there on and off. Perched on a hill in Twin Peaks, in San Francisco, the four-story modern home had a view of the city skyline. With white minimal décor, spiral staircase, Spartan leather couches, electric fireplace, a pile of sneakers in the entryway, and dorm-like tapestries, it looked like a scene out of *Home Alone*. But instead of throwing frat parties, TheGlint housemates philosophized for fun.

At that time, along with Burnham, Kiselev, and Lim, lived Tom Currier, a twenty-year-old who was awarded a Thiel Fellowship for making his father's Porsche electric. He launched his own company called Black Swan Solar, where he had developed a heliostat, or "death ray," that bounced sunlight to one central point and could ultimately be used as an alternative source of energy.

TheGlint turned out to be a major connector for the fellows, especially Burnham. There, he met a friend, Greg Ryan, who convinced him to abandon his asteroid mining plans and to instead help him start a company that would convert cash into commodities and allow customers to purchase items with gold.

It was John's first "pivot": the tech term for scrapping your current idea, as in moving from mining asteroids to creating an app to pay in gold. "The space industry," he said, "is not the most conducive to entrepreneurship, and I'm not the right person to do the idea."

Burnham said that through their commodities app, he and Ryan would make currency irrelevant. "You could in practice buy coffee with gold," he explained, once they had set up their app, which they named Daric. "The reason to do this is, you don't want to store your money in fiat currency, given the current policy of quantitative easing." John had just turned nineteen a few weeks ago. It fit right into his libertarian ideology. "Storing your money in dollars is actually quite dangerous." Burnham's company would issue its customers debit cards for their Daric bank accounts. The merchant would be paid in cash, and Daric would deduct the same amount in gold from the user's account. The eventual user base would trade gold with one another.

Burnham said he had been interested in commodities for a long time. "I was sitting on my father's IT desk freshman year of high school," he recalled. "My interest in asteroid mining really came out of my interest in finance." Stephen Burnham was an executive at Marco Polo Securities, an online private equity exchange for emerging markets. "My dad's version of homeschooling was 'You're going to work at my company and learn a lot of math and read a lot of books,'" said Burnham. "I think I did the equivalent of three and a half years of math in freshman year." By the following year, young John had flipped through the AP economics textbook and thought, "This is lame; it doesn't tell you any of the cool stuff." At TheGlint, he had found a kindred spirit in Ryan.

TheGlint was hardly the only co-living house in Silicon Valley designed to foster ideas and blend work and life. These shared pseudodormitories—without adult supervision, of course—had become so popular in Silicon Valley that some companies started offering networking nights consisting of "innovation mansion tours." Tropo, a cloud communications company, took its customers on a "progressive"—a term usually used to describe a frat party's progression from one specialty drink to another in different dorm rooms down the hallway—to three of the local mansions.

In addition to TheGlint, there was Factory Zero, a San Francisco townhouse where members of the early seed venture capital firm Memento lived; and the Villa, a ten-thousand-square-foot mansion in the Noe Valley neighborhood.

The Silicon Valley Start-up Mansion Crawl started with a barbecue and pool party at the Villa. From there tourgoers took the bus to TheGlint for drinks and dessert, before winding up at Factory Zero for wine and cheese.

Down in Palo Alto, another group of Thiel fellows was experimenting with its own home. Near the late Apple CEO Steve Jobs's house in Palo Alto, past Google founder Larry Page's California Arts and Crafts $7.95 million mansion, is a seventeen-thousand-square-foot English Tudor–style house covered in vines and buttressed by a fuchsia flower garden surrounding a pool. A lone grey SUV sat out front. Every now and then a teenager with a backpack and glasses walked out of the arched doorway, got on a bike or a scooter, and rode past mothers and fathers walking their dogs, or couples driving to and from work. At that corner house, however, the parents didn't live there.

During that first summer of the Thiel Fellowship, seven lived in one of these co-living homes at the intersection of Santa Rita Avenue and Cowper Street. After months of searching for affordable housing on Craigslist, they stumbled upon this 1920s five-bedroom house with all its period accoutrements, from butler doors to dumbwaiters. They all worked on different company ideas. Four of the boys, Sebastien Zany, Darren Zhu, David Merfield, and Nick Cammarata, all moved here with Laura Deming, the native New Zealander who "wants to extend the human lifespan for a few centuries—at the very least." Ben Yu joined them a few months later. Some of the fellows roomed together in the upstairs bedrooms, while others squeezed into the garage and the pool house. They divided the $5,500 rent until May 2012, when the owner wanted to put the property on the market for $5 million.

As of late October 2011, though, they still hadn't finished furnishing it. Instead, they sparsely and somewhat haphazardly decorated the downstairs with laptops and whiteboards, making the house function as more of an office than a home. On the mantel facing a long wraparound couch was not a television but a big-screen computer monitor.

"It keeps us focused," said Zhu, referring to the lack of television. Farther down the hall was the dining room, where they used the long dinner table for meetings. Zhu and Luan, cofounders of Dextro, a robotics company that would build robots to automate the biotech industry, both wore glasses, jeans, and striped polo shirts. The two, who first met as Yale sophomores, decided to work together after being accepted as fellows.

They had covered one wall with dry-erase boards, which they'd filled with algorithmic designs for robot creation and outlines for business development strategies.

The seven of them created a minifamily, and in this house,

they showed off the life they had built together. We walked around the corner to the kitchen, where they opened the fridge to show that it was fully stocked with sausages, vegetables, pasta, fruit, and loaves of bread from Whole Foods. The fellows cooked most nights rather than eat out or get takeout. "We're trying to stretch the money as much as possible," said Luan.

The kitchen led outside to a brick-covered patio that looked out to the pool house, where Zany lived. "Sebastien has his own suite out here!" exclaimed Zhu. Zany would soon spackle the walls with supplies from Home Depot and hang up posters and tapestries, turning the small structure into an airy dorm room. The next building over was the garage, containing bikes, scooters—and a grand piano. When a mentor dropped off the piano before he moved houses, the fellows couldn't believe it. "We got someone to give us a piano and have it delivered!" Zhu said excitedly.

Upstairs, Merfield and Cammarata lived and worked out of their bedroom. Luan and Zhu occupied the sprawling master suite in the middle of the floor. Although they'd been living in the house for more than a month, David had just discovered that his four-hundred-square-foot bedroom had a balcony, though he still hadn't been out on it. "It's pretty great," he said. "We keep finding things in this house we never knew were there."

As the only girl, Deming had her own room next door. Laura, working part-time at a lab, was having trouble coming up with funding for her proposed longevity private equity fund. She had no shortage of mentors willing to meet with her, but she didn't have a business partner who could help run the financials of her company. She preferred to spend her time with mice in the labs than with most of the men who had tried to date her under the guise of investment. Deming, like the other fellows, had a command of her field unusual for her age and sex, as well as an unusual obsession with it. She fit in well at Silicon Valley's many happy hours, where companies hosted employee after-work events more regularly than the staff socialized on its own. When the Thiel House's owner announced he was looking to sell, Deming started socializing more, to see if she could find a new living situation.

At one of these, at former Google CEO Eric Schmidt's venture firm Innovation Endeavors, she met Julia Lipton leaning against a balcony rail sipping San Pellegrino. Pert and petite, Lipton, twenty-two, looked out over the city of Palo Alto, where she had lived for a year while working at Quixey, a search engine for apps. She was at one of a handful of these happy hours that she attends each week for networking purposes with her start-up house roommates. The following night, her boss, Quixey founder Liron Shapira, would host a happy hour for college kids to encourage them to stop out of school and work for him. "At least that's the subtext," Lipton said. Shapira dropped out of college himself to launch his own company, "and he encourages people to learn computer science not in the classroom but by starting a start-up," she explained.

As with many twenty-somethings who moved to Silicon Valley, Lipton's work and social life had become one. She spent most of her time at the "Quixeyplex," the one-story Palo Alto building where colorful stickers of apps such as YouTube, Skype, and Twitter cover walls and staircases. Lipton ended up there after graduating from the University of Southern California and then interning at Merrill Lynch and Accenture—"pretty standard jobs," as she recalled. In college, she had studied with engineers and found that she and they seemed more excited about programming than about partying. So for senior year spring break, instead of going with her friends to Cancún, Mexico, Lipton flew out to Silicon Valley and scheduled meetings with interesting people she had found on LinkedIn. There she met with entrepreneur Adam Rifkin, who offered her the in-house public relations and marketing role she has now. By March, Lipton had relocated to Palo Alto, where she moved in with another start-up staffer and soon adapted to the techie schedule.

Tonight Lipton wasn't drinking. After all, she had to go back to work. She did, however, sample some of the start-up diet-friendly cuisine, slicing a piece of manchego cheese to pair with Marcona almonds. All purchased from Whole Foods, there was nary a refined carbohydrate in sight—or possibly even in the building. The natural, organic fast-food joint Lyfe

Kitchen occupied the ground floor and had become an official canteen for tech offices along University Avenue. So prevalent was the gastronomically aware engineer, that area restaurants had entire menu pages designated to these healthful new start-up habits.

The houses reinforced those habits—healthful and otherwise. The Villa would become the backdrop of the reality show *Silicon Valley*. Produced by Mark Zuckerberg's sister Randi Zuckerberg, along with the same team that made the *Den of Thieves* TV series and the MTV Video Music Awards, *Silicon Valley* followed five mansion dwellers trying to build billion-dollar companies as they party and conference hop their way through the Bay Area. Two cast members, brother and sister Benjamin and Hermione Way, lived in the Villa, where they worked on their media start-ups. Hermione, who calls herself a "vlogger," or video blogger, wrote for the tech website The Next Web. Her brother started a company at age fifteen that raised $50 million. This show was the precursor to an HBO comedy series also called *Silicon Valley*. Although it wasn't a reality show, it looked like one. With characters resembling Thiel, Sergey Brin, and the TechCrunch Disrupt conference's Michael Arrington, many Silicon Valley dwellers thought it could have been a documentary.

Their house was an imitation of Zuckerberg's Palo Alto home in *The Social Network*. But others like it had existed before in one form or another. One of the first was Rainbow Mansion, started in 2006 by Chris Kemp, then NASA's chief technology officer, and other NASA employees looking to share rides and costs. The sprawling abode had been home to some fifty tech employees over the last few years. Though the early mansion dwellers were from NASA, within a few months they started recruiting people from Apple and Google, as well as students from Stanford. It became the first of these communal living homes with shared rent in which inhabitants work, eat, and play together.

"We figured the Bay Area had lots of giant mansions and we thought we'd find one on Craigslist," remembered Kemp, a slim thirty-nine-year-old with spiky hair, clear blue eyes, and thin-framed glasses. Few had cars, so they figured living together would be a more efficient way to get to work. When they found a property big enough at the right price—an eighteen-room Spanish-tiled mansion on Rainbow Drive in Palo Alto—it was already furnished with 1990s-style décor, a grand piano, and a personal theater. Five of the first group of eight who would live there pooled the funds for the first and last month's security deposit, totaling $50,000. The only downside was that with so many people in such a large house, they ended up in the highest bracket for power and water consumption. Also, neighbors did not appreciate the parties the house would regularly have for hundreds of company employees. Still, the housemates stayed. They liked being able to hold spontaneous salons where they would talk about work and ideas.

When Celestine Johnson first arrived in the area, she too lived in Rainbow Mansion. Now she was hovering in Eric Schmidt's orbit. For many newbies, gravitating toward a kingpin was a reliable path forward. He was hers, and she had infiltrated the world of Innovation Endeavors, in part through her co-living communities.

Johnson had been working on the Corporate Social Responsibility team at Apple, looking after Supplier Responsibility, or human rights and the environment. When she walked into Rainbow Mansion, she found eight male roommates watching the nature documentary series *Planet Earth* under a five-by-five-foot tetrahedron built out of paper towel rolls hanging from the ceiling. Scattered around the living room were telescopes belonging to a few of the guys who worked at NASA. Then there was the didgeridoo that one of them had fashioned out of sugarcane.

Johnson had discovered this Cupertino co-living community by answering a Craigslist ad seeking a roommate who would want to "join an intellectual community to change the world." After a series of phone interviews with housemates who asked her what she was doing to change the world, and how and why she planned to do it, and then an in-person interview, Johnson was offered her own room. It had sleek, new wood floors. The house was crowded, but noise wouldn't be a problem. Her housemate in the next room had turned his into a meditation room equipped with raised flooring and tatami mats. "I think I was in the maid's room," she recalled. "But it was a reasonably sized room"—especially compared with the master bedroom, which at one point had four people living in it, including one in the closet.

With occupants ranging from their late teens to their midthirties, the $5 million houses full of telescopes, terminals, and other high-tech toys, and everything from pools to motes to koi ponds, were veritable MTV *Real World* mansions, except they boasted whiteboards instead of flat-screens. The male-to-female ratio was nearly 10:1.

This new surge in communal living intensified as Facebook and Google started growing in the mid-aughts, and Silicon Valley companies and venture capital firms encouraged their employees to live and code together. Paul Graham's incubator Y Combinator gave entrepreneurs seed money on the basis that the employees live near where they work, bringing new young talent to the valley every year. Based on this model, investors and tech companies started using housing as a place not just for beds but also for brainstorming.

So far, Google, Innovation Endeavors, and a string of venture capital firms along Sand Hill Road had their engineers in co-living communities such as the Blackbox Mansion, a shingled, traditional family home on the outside that could be booked only through Airbnb, the online housing and vacation rental site, and

the actual DevHouse, an event company, named after this phenomenon, that sets up networking events for techies. UpWest
Labs, an Israeli seed fund, and Innovation Endeavors organized
their live-work spaces as incubators for company ideas.

Business rules were stringent ("Attend meetings for which
you sign up. Cancel with staff if you will not be able to attend")
while interpersonal rules were often written in casual college-like
vernacular ("Residents may not enter into each other's rooms unless they are invited by a resident of that room").

Leadership and nightly chef duty often remained self-
selecting. Every night after a big Costco shopping run to stock
the Sub-Zero fridge, which soon multiplied as the house filled
up, entrepreneurs would take turns volunteering for kitchen
duty. Former NASA employee Kemp said the task usually fell
to the vegan or vegetarian housemates who wanted to make
sure "no one throws hunks of cow on the grill." For the first
few years, Kemp was the house leader, but then new people
started to take over. "The most interesting people were the last
you'd want to remind to pay the rent on time," he recalled, "so
by being the most responsible person, I was actually the least
interesting."

After converting the second-floor media room into a hostel,
they let friends of friends and area interns use the space, while
entrepreneurs unable to afford the monthly rent could crash on
futons or bunk beds. "Economics were not the driving factor of

the house," said Kemp. If guests were creative and added to the house's culture, they might not have to pay as much. Rather than asking can they afford it, Kemp's questions were always "Are these people doing something important?" and "Are they going to add to the character and the experience of the house?"

Kemp figured that if the multiple-family-home idea did not work out, he would try to create a home for employees based in the area for weeks at a time. He hoped to build a sort of temporary community of rotating entrepreneurs, envisioning a giant house where different people would have private rooms where they could leave their belongings. "They'd have a sense of community but also more privacy and a more culturally rich space," said Kemp.

So far, though, the government was not making it easy. When Google tried to build a company-sponsored community designed around colleague collaboration close to its campus, the city rejected the plan. But even though having Google house its staff in its own residential village didn't get past the local government, there was nothing the city could do about the employees organizing their own living situations that way. For entrepreneurs to take the risks involved in starting a company—often for low pay and a high amount of faith—living together served to reinforce their commitment to a company cause that often, by sane standards, would never exist. Long hours at work with little relief in terms of social activity almost *forced* work to be viewed as fun.

Because the willingness to live together was already apparent in the area, Kemp thought there would be room to expand what he'd built at the Rainbow Mansion. In the meantime, a new Silicon Valley status quo had emerged out of his original vision: now the first stop after getting a job was often a co-living community. But for housemates in all of these mansions, the realities of co-living could prove to be overly alternative. In 2009, after living in Rainbow Mansion for a year and a half, Celestine Johnson moved into a live-and-work house in Woodside that she said was full of interesting engineers and physicists, plus gardens, their own chickens, and house-brewed beer—but that was about it. Eventually she moved to San Francisco, for the reason that these live-work mansions exist: "All we did in Cupertino was Rainbow Mansion; there are limited options for young people to go in Silicon Valley."

Meanwhile, the live-work concept would continue to evolve. Johnson and Chris Kemp started working on the idea of developing crash pads in Palo Alto for venture capitalists, company employees, and founders to stay when they are too tired to commute back to San Francisco. And one of their other housemates, Jessy Schlinger, a woman who moved into Rainbow Mansion a few months into Johnson's tenure there, took up that mantle for the most part and was now starting a new network of entrepreneurial mansions called Embassy Network. Langton Labs's Todd Huffman sent her people to fill some of the houses if they didn't fit into his space. "She's one of the go-to people for collaborative living," said Johnson. Schlinger just took over an old monastery in San Francisco and installed a bowling alley in the basement.

In a way, these share houses were still just a later stage of the hippy living tradition that the Bay Area had long been known for. But this time, the captains of industry were leading the charge. If psychedelic drugs once put people in a collective trance in the 1960s, these days that drug was the ephemeral motto of "changing the world"—which, when translated into East Coast, meant "changing the wallet," to make it much fatter in as little time as possible.

By 2012, John Burnham's own wallet was getting slim. He had gone through practically all his grant money in his first few months, so he had to move back down to Silicon Valley: to a small studio in Mountain View, about ten minutes south of the Thiel fellows' house on Santa Rita.

Still, he said he was making strides at his new company, Daric, by working on it remotely from his home in Mountain View, writing algorithms for the back end of his business. He would occasionally travel back east to meet with company advisors (when his parents bought him a plane ticket home). He said he had convinced business leaders such as Jennifer Johnson, co-president at the investment management firm Franklin

Templeton, and Kenneth Chenault, CEO of American Express, to advise the company.

"We've met with CEOs of every major credit card company," Burnham announced proudly. He paused. "I know, right?" He took a swig of coffee. "We just have fantastic connections, right?" he asked rhetorically. In a way, he sounded like he was trying to convince himself. Strung out and exhausted from the stresses of adult life, such as rent, budgeting, laundry, and transportation, he was trying to keep it together. "We're not ragtag," he insisted.

But Burnham was struggling once again, especially socially. He wanted some more friends nearby and a lot more excitement. So he went back to Patri Friedman and Danielle Strachman at the Thiel Fellowship and asked how he could be more involved with the other fellows. They were already hard at work selecting the next class of fellows and offered him a chance to help find new candidates. As he advised the mentees, one of them caught his eye. Her name was Noor Siddiqui.

4

The Never-Ending School

By fall 2012, John Burnham was living in Mountain View, spending his time reading novels he would have read if he were in college, such as Ernest Hemingway's *A Farewell to Arms* and the ancient epic poem *The Aeneid* by Virgil. He heard that Peter Thiel was going to begin guest lecturing at Stanford University. Titled "Start-up," and offered through the computer science department, Thiel's course was open to pretty much anyone who could find a parking spot on campus or who was flexible enough to sit cross-legged jammed up next to other pairs of crossed legs in the auditorium's aisles.

From the first class, the room overflowed with attendees, not all of them students. Only 250 people could fit into the auditorium, so ten minutes before Thiel's lecture on "Secrets," which later became the title of a chapter in his 2014 book *Zero to One: Notes on Startups, or How to Build the Future*, the hallway was full as well. Students—and adults who looked like they had been students decades ago but still dressed like them—covered the walls and the paths leading down to the stage.

Finally, after all this buildup, Thiel walked across the stage in front of a screen broadcasting his course's title with cinematic grandeur. The crowd became quiet, and he started talking about how secrets are impossible to find, and how most good companies started because somebody stumbled on a secret. The audience listened attentively, writing down Thiel's pointers as if the entrepreneur were giving away his own secrets. If they came up with a good enough company idea, maybe he'd fund it, just like investor Peter Gregory, the character unmistakably modeled after him on the hit HBO show *Silicon Valley*.

In the front row, in full view of his benefactor, sat Burnham. He was probably one of the few audience members not taking notes. After all, he went only for the "face time," and the notes were already online. One of Thiel's pupils, a Stanford law student named Blake Masters, would transcribe and annotate all of his lectures, which would eventually become *Zero to One*. The book would go up against that Silicon Valley book of books, the bridge from the small silo of the tech company c-suite to mainstream success: Sheryl Sandberg's bestselling *Lean In: Women, Work, and the Will to Lead*. She had made it not only to the apex of power in the Bay Area, but also to the apex of power as a woman, a writer, and, in some circles, a philosopher—and perhaps someday a politician, many people thought. Thiel, however, wanted to write a different kind of book, one not nearly as politically correct. His book would rail against all that.

But back then, this class was just a class, and among his pupils were several Thiel fellows. Ironically, while Thiel's educational credentials came from Stanford, he taught there, and he funded its students, he was also spearheading a program that questioned everything for which it stood. It was a question often asked in interviews: whether or not he regretted having gone to Stanford and getting a college education and a law degree there. He would always respond that he did not regret it at all, and that for someone like him—with his level of intelligence, and faced with the options he had at the time—he would do the exact same thing. Now, though, the world was different. Perhaps he would make a different choice.

The fellows in the room had taken that new option, yet here they were back in a college auditorium. And it was Burnham's event of the week. He went to Stanford parties and tried to find Stanford friends. Later fellows would work out of the Center for Entrepreneurial Studies at Stanford. The university, after all, had started it all and helped make Silicon Valley in large part what it is today. That same spring, Thiel wasn't the only Silicon Valley luminary on campus. Near his lecture hall on the third floor of the Jen-Hsun Huang Engineering Center—Yahoo CEO Marissa Mayer, LinkedIn cofounder Reid Hoffman, Instagram cofounder Mike Krieger, and Quora cofounder Charlie Cheever would come back to campus to celebrate the twenty-fifth anniversary of their undergraduate major, Symbolic Systems. The academic program had produced nearly fifty entrepreneurs whose companies went on to make billions. Since then, with organizations such as the Stanford Computer Forum, which aligned area tech companies with Stanford research, to the university's Institute of Design (or d.school) to the forty-plus entrepreneurship courses on offer and the multiple venture capital, private equity, and iPhone-app clubs, Stanford had become a hotbed, if not the engine, of start-up mania.

A few months after Thiel's "Secrets" seminar, an actual secret event was being held, without students flooding in. It was the second day of the Symbolic Systems conference, where "Sym-Sys" majors and alumni were honoring the Stanford-specific program that explored cognitive science, artificial intelligence, and human-computer interaction. It was a liberal sciences parallel to the liberal arts: Sym-Sys students took courses in a range of disciplines, including computer science, linguistics, philosophy, and psychology. Over the program's twenty-five-year history, a significant percentage of its seven hundred alumni had gone on to become tech leading lights, and today, executives from Silicon Valley's hottest companies—the valuations in this room alone ranged from $1 billion to $200 billion—were paying tribute at the lectern.

The small audience was low-key, and there were no video cameras or flashes. Cheever and Powerset founder Barney Pell, a Thiel fellow mentor, sat near Hoffman. They watched their fellow majors talk about what they'd gotten out of the program. Apple senior vice president Scott Forstall noted that his Sym-Sys studies "convinced me we could build a simple touch keyboard that would work well." He closed his speech by saying, "I guess this is a long-winded answer to give credit to Symbolic Systems for the creation of the iPhone and the iPad."

Mayer, at the time Google's vice president of local, maps, and location services before she left to run Yahoo, soon got up and said the only reason she was chosen to work on the company's user interface was that her boss saw that she had taken psychology, a Sym-Sys requirement. Another class, the infamously difficult Philosophy 160A, she said, "gave me a lot of confidence when we were in crunch time" during Google's early days.

Later in the day, Michael Krieger stood at the podium and announced that every job he'd ever had, including founding Instagram, had been because of his Stanford major. It was how he met his eventual cofounder, Kevin Systrom. The two became

Mayfield Fellows together, part of a selective work-study program run by Stanford's Technology Ventures Program. They
made contacts in industry and could thus raise key venture capital
money. "I think of Symbolic Systems as the ideal entrepreneur's
degree," he said.

Krieger's claim seemed like it was becoming more and more
true for both those who had graduated from the school and those
who had not. Whether Stanford fueled the tech explosion or the
industry made Stanford more prominent was a chicken-or-egg
question dating back more than a century. The first major tech
company in the area, Federal Telegraph, was founded by a Stanford grad in 1909, making the region a leader in the development
of radio vacuum tubes. Then, in 1937, Stanford graduates Bill
Hewlett and David Packard started Hewlett-Packard, the success of which spawned dozens of other tech companies in the
following years. In the 1950s, the semiconductor inventor William Shockley moved to the area looking for engineers to work
on a new transistor, and members of his staff went on to start
Fairchild Semiconductor.

While most schools transitioned from regional renown to
national prestige through an undefeated athletic team, one of
Stanford's great prizes was arguably its computer science department. Started in 1965 by professor emeritus and former provost William Miller, it was the first program at the university to
work closely with industry. In 1968 Miller created the Stanford

Computer Forum, which allowed companies such as Cisco, Sun Microsystems, and General Electric to get an early look at Stanford student research. "That was the beginning of the strong interactions between the computer science department and industry," Miller reflected. "It's become much more intensified since then, particularly in the last fifteen years."

With the introduction of the first Web browsers in the early 1990s, the Internet had Silicon Valley booming. And it was two Stanford computer science grad students, Sergey Brin and Larry Page, who developed one of the most successful and significant companies of the Internet era: Google.

Then came the dot.com bust of 1999, a speculative bubble in which the prices of many new technology companies were largely inflated, and eventually burst. It was in those first years after the crash, when the world thought tech was dead, that the groundwork for start-up mania was laid. New open-source technology made building a website affordable. By the mid-aughts, the average cost of starting an Internet company had dropped from $5 million to $500,000, thanks to a combination of factors. First, larger companies such as Yahoo and Google opened their programming interfaces to others; then the front-end revolution made web pages less static; and, finally, bandwidth expanded rapidly. The founding of the blogging platform WordPress.com alone, in 2003, launched millions of new websites within a matter of years.

Fueling much of this rapidly improving technology were Stanford engineers. "Stanford is really one of the engines that drives the tech industry," said Toni Schneider, CEO of Automattic, the company that owns WordPress. "It is this constant injection of new people and new ideas and research." At the same time, Stanford has allowed a "tech transfer," letting companies that were created on campus, such as Google, into the marketplace. "It had a pioneering role for universities being open to commercialization of ideas," said Schneider.

Some of the area's most successful start-up accelerators, including Stanford's own StartX, were founded by students. Y Combinator, the seed-stage funding firm that incubated Dropbox and Airbnb, was venture capitalist Paul Graham's way to encourage students to start companies, rather than take internships, during school breaks. And angel investor Dave McClure's venture fund and seed accelerator 500 Startups grew out of an app development class he taught at Stanford.

Students who started companies at Stanford tended to stay in Silicon Valley, reinforcing the cross-fertilization between campus and community. In a place where the rates of colossal failure and exponential success are so extreme they cancel out each other, the flat line between them represents the slope of the barrier to entry. Former provost Miller says that Stanford stands out because it teaches its students that it's okay to try and fail. "People are willing to experiment, and that creates this open attitude," he observed.

It is that attitude that Tim Westergren said led him to co-found the music recommendation service Pandora Radio, now valued at $3.5 billion. After his Stanford graduation, Westergren took a job as a nanny so he would have time to produce and write music on the side. It was the best decision he ever made, he said, crediting a Stanford class on organizational decision making and leadership for convincing him to stick with what he loved to do. "The objective in these classes," he reflected, "was a think-for-yourself approach to life." Westergren also applauded the technical bent that former Stanford president John Hennessy had brought to the community. "Now a generation of entrepreneurs who have gone into semiretirement are looking to come back to Stanford and teach," he said.

After Eric Schmidt stepped down as Google's CEO in 2011, he did just that. And when he met a bright young Israeli student in his venture capital entrepreneurship class, he hired him at the end of the semester. Dror Berman, thirty-three, started running Schmidt's firm Innovation Endeavors in 2010. "All my classmates became entrepreneurs," said Berman. So far, he has funded over fifty companies, many of them founded by Stanford friends.

The university was well aware of the networking opportunity it had become. In 1997 Professor Tom Byers started the Stanford Technology Ventures Program, an entrepreneur center that included resources, seminars, conference programming, and the prestigious Mayfield Fellows Program. Instagram cofounders Krieger and Systrom were among the select few who got in. "It is the Navy SEALs of entrepreneurship," according to Byers, in the lower level of the engineering school, where the Entrepreneurship Center was based.

Back at the Symbolic Systems conference, as Krieger finished his presentation, passersby had caught on to the fact that Silicon Valley celebrities were here that day. Soon the room swelled with people eager to hear his advice. All the while, the question looming was whether the billion-dollar sale of his photo-sharing app was a sign of another bubble yet to come, one encompassing Stanford's very campus. But in a place where entrepreneurship is encouraged and failure is accepted, many students asked instead, what would have been the worst thing that could've happened if they'd left school to start a company that flopped? They would have come back and graduated, that's what.

There were plenty of professors on campus hoping that would be the case. They didn't advocate failure per se, but, rather, the need for a college education and the idea that graduation shouldn't be something to take for granted. During the early years of the Thiel Fellowship, one of Peter's staunchest detractors was Carnegie Mellon University professor Vivek Wadhwa. With columns in the *Washington Post* and *Bloomberg Businessweek*, Wadhwa had a wide mouthpiece in the mainstream media—which he used to bash Thiel frequently. Wadhwa eventually debated him and the writer Charles Murray, coauthor of the controversial 1994 book *The Bell Curve: Intelligence and Class Structure in American Life*, in Chicago to argue against the idea that "Too Many Kids Are Going to College."

Wadhwa, a stout, jolly entrepreneur turned professor had roles at Stanford, Duke, and Singularity Universities, the latter a school full of Thiel fellow mentors that researches artificial intelligence and longevity, among other tech-focused topics. The professor also authored a book called *The Immigrant Exodus: Why America Is Losing the Global Race to Capture Entrepreneurial Talent*." The main reason, he argues, is because of our diminishing education standards.

His *Washington Post* columns, along with journalist Jacob Weisberg's pieces in *Slate*, were some of the harshest voices in the media against Thiel and his 20 Under 20 Fellowship. Cheerful and smiling during the Chicago debate, Wadhwa wanted the audience to like him. "I've been researching what's been happening globally. I've been researching the impact of globalization on US competitiveness," he said, opening his arms toward the crowd. "These people in America are totally, completely out of touch . . . We don't get it. . . . We're sitting here in our own bubble disconnected from the rest of the world." Wadhwa explained that because education in the United States was the best in the world, other countries were trying to replicate it, and students came to

America to learn how to be like us. He cited the Chinese and the Indians, who, in his opinion, had in effect learned to beat their teachers by educating themselves in America.

"I've faced stereotypes," he said. "My people were beggars and snake charmers, then we became low-level engineers, and now we're hotshot CEOs." Now, he said, Indians were more motivated than ever to bring everyone up to the same level through American education. "The Indians and Chinese are going to be eating our children's lunch, guaranteed."

Thiel fired back. "The US—there are about forty percent college-aged students in college," he replied. "In China, the number is twenty percent. In India, the number is ten percent, so it's a brutally selective system . . . if we want to be more like them, far fewer people should go to college." Thiel said Wadhwa's argument was a powerful one for *his* side.

Wadhwa, however, just smiled at the crowd and looked away from the table where Thiel sat next to his debate partner, Charles Murray. He opened his arms again to the audience. Then he grinned and said, "I would educate everyone in the world because it uplifts society."

Wadhwa continued his public arguments with Thiel for the next few months. He even had a "cage match" with Thiel fellow Dale Stephens at the Long Beach TED Conference. There Stephens argued the benefits of his program UnCollege: a system of teaching oneself that turned into a book and "Hackademic

Camp," in which Stephens organized a week for invited campers to learn and practice why they should be teaching themselves
versus going to college.

By summer 2012, Stephens's UnCollege movement had picked
up almost as much notoriety as the Thiel Fellowship. That August, the twenty-year-old college dropout was presiding over two
long picnic tables on the back patio of a five-bedroom townhouse
in the Haight-Ashbury neighborhood in San Francisco. He had
rented the house on Airbnb for his Hackademic Camp, for which
he had recruited fifteen aspiring entrepreneurs to attend a week
of seminars and workshops on how to drop out of college. They
looked like college kids, dressed in jeans, shorts, and T-shirts, carried laptops and were obedient students, but they were there to
test what it would be like not to go back to school. Stephens went
from huddle to huddle, asking with camp counselor enthusiasm
whether they were more convinced to teach themselves going
forward. He had arranged panels, speakers, and company visits
to inspire his campers.

They had another five minutes until their next speaker arrived, so they started to pack up their containers of quinoa and
veggie chips and drank the last sips of their Kombucha teas.
Stephens, in pale-grey fitted jeans and a loose boat-neck yellow
T-shirt, directed the group of twenty-somethings down the stairs
to the lower level of the house, where backpacks were strewn

about a makeshift conference table. Signs of sleep the night before were visible through a door in the back of the room, where air mattresses and crumpled sheets were crammed against the wall.

The first speaker of the afternoon was a software engineer and early Facebook employee named Todd Perry, who wore the Silicon Valley uniform of thick-rimmed, black-framed glasses, jeans, and a grey T-shirt. He didn't look much different from his audience, who wore the same kind of outfit, just slightly hipper versions, with ripped jean shorts on the men, lower-cut tank tops on the women, and various shavings and piercings.

The blue curtains blocking the view of the patio looked as though they had been pasted on the windows with Elmer's glue and were about to fall. But Perry didn't use the slide projector, so he didn't mind the brightness. He was talking to the group about how everyone should forget college and learn to program instead. Perry ended up at Facebook because he'd met Mark Zuckerberg at Phillips Exeter Academy in New Hampshire, a boarding school, where he was Zuckerberg's teaching assistant. The campers, who were all chugging blue energy drinks and caffeinated soda and clacking away on their laptops, gasped.

Perry, who left the company two years before the IPO, started by asking their thoughts on the relevance of the famous social network. "Facebook has replaced business cards," said a young man named Simon. "All you need is a name." Next was Celine, who said, "We use Facebook mostly for cheating." Perry laughed. "We post answers in groups." Perry was particularly interested in those who said Facebook was over. Considering that he quit before getting his million-dollar payoff, Perry seemed somewhat bitter. It turned out, he left to become a female lounge singer named Suzy. Despite appearing with a straight, Asperger's-chic quality today, he dressed up as his blonde-wigged alter ego in the evenings.

Now Perry was describing his path to Silicon Valley. His interest in Nintendo and then Final Fantasy, a science-fiction video game that any self-respecting engineer seemed to have grown up playing, was a common route to coding. He passed around his early journals to show how he learned to program. They documented how he first taught himself by figuring out how the video game Super Mario Bros. was built. When Perry got to his stint at Facebook, he focused on his admiration for Mark Zuckerberg and what qualities it took to make him who he was today. "Zuck was doing the Lean Startup for years in middle school," he explained, referring to entrepreneur Eric Ries's program for building a start-up without much overhead and iterating on your idea until you get it right. He explained that everything about the Facebook founder and CEO, from his *Star Wars*–themed bar mitzvah to his participation on the fencing team and the math contest club, represented the iterative way that Zuckerberg's mind worked. Perry then described how Mark's favorite math teacher at Exeter used to forbid his students to use calculators, and anyone who had to use one was forced to do push-ups. Zuckerberg decided to write code for all his homework and just do the push-ups anyway. "He still got into Harvard," Perry said, laughing.

The ability to code gave these engineers, who in large groups remained quiet unless asked a specific question based on their expertise, a confidence that they were more highly developed than other people. They possessed a cockiness unexpected from computer science geeks. If you couldn't program, you couldn't speak their language. In that sense, Perry said, the 2010 film *The Social Network* was an accurate portrayal of what happened, especially in the nerd-versus-frat competition. In 2005, when the good-looking, crew-rowing Winklevoss twins, Cameron and Tyler, were trying to combat the more technologically savvy competition of Facebook, they wrote a program to scrape the email addresses Facebook had already signed up. Zuckerberg took the program as an attack and spent all night writing a JavaScript obfuscator to break the Winklevi's—how the Mark Zuckerberg character jokingly refers to the Winklevoss twins, as though Winklevi (pronounced "winkle-vie") is the plural of a Latin -us ending—code. He launched it at three in the morning and then went to Jack in the Box for hamburgers. That was the quality of Zuckerberg's that the Oscar-nominated film missed, according to Perry, because it made Zuckerberg all about business. "The movie banned the trait that made him successful: his ability to find humor in code."

As a leader, Zuckerberg didn't feel confident running Facebook until 2006, when he refused to sell it for a billion dollars, explained Perry. "He was not a good motivational leader but led by example. Then in 2006 Viacom was offering to fly him everywhere, and he took all the meetings, upset all the people, and in parallel released the newsfeed feature"—a continual stream of updates that was controversial at first among users. But within Facebook, it made a statement. "From then on, he was the leader of Facebook," said Perry.

When it came time for questions and answers, the campers, trying out what it would be like to "hack" their own education, wanted to know what they could do to be like Zuckerberg if they hadn't started coding at age ten. Perry said it was never too late and that now, with the rise of digital media, "even humanities people need to know how to code. Programming makes you sharper and prevents you getting old and rigid. It's more like creative writing than it used to be."

After Perry was done, the group had a five-minute recess before the second session. The campers checked their email, and then ran upstairs to make coffee and take a bathroom break in the marble-tiled ground-floor facility equipped with an oversize Jacuzzi.

The next stop was a visit to IGN Entertainment Games, a gaming company that had organized a meet-and-greet with the dropouts over pizza in its office in San Francisco's SoMa, or South of Market (Street) area. The group broke up into four different cars. Some jumped into a bright-blue Prius they'd picked up behind aluminum fencing at a City Car Share lot.

Despite a few wrong turns, they ended up on Brannan Street and arrived at IGN. Elevators brought them up to life-size mannequins of Alien versus Predator and other video game characters. After the Hackademic Camp group waited in a lounge area strewn with arcade games and vending machines that sold healthy treats (all baked, not fried) for only twenty-five cents, they were greeted by a team called Code Foo. The mostly Asian interns explained their rotating six-week training program coding for the company. Meanwhile, the campers, including students from prestigious colleges such as UC Berkeley and Yale University, glanced around at the video games on the wall and eyed the front door for the pizza delivery man. Code Foo even accepted college dropouts—or anyone who could impress IGN with his or her engineering skills. The recruitment ad for the program read: "Flipping burgers to scrape together enough cash to buy *Portal 2*? Blow our minds while you're here, and we'll hire you." Those accepted would spend six weeks programming and then another six weeks learning the core competencies needed to work there full-time. If they could show they were up to the task, IGN would hire them.

Just before the two sides of IGN staffers and campers broke the divide like at a high school dance, a manager ran up and realized they had brought out kegs of beer even though most of the campers were under twenty-one. They quickly removed them.

5

The All-Meat Lunch

Underage guests were a recurring problem at the Silicon Valley happy hours. To find the youngest untapped talent, companies often looked for employees to pluck far before their pre-freshman weekends. Many recruiters didn't want to wait until students started college, let alone graduated. Android, the mobile operating system, paid students to hand out Android pajamas to their friends. Tech recruiting firms sent letters to talented engineers urging them to leave school to work for start-ups, just as the NFL would recruit a promising football player. From free food, to company T-shirts, to six-figure starting salaries, early hires leaving school were incentivized not only in the short term but also with equity in the fledgling companies they might be leaving school to join. These days, instead of Wall Street investment banks taking out their summer interns to steak houses and strip clubs—the frattastic havens of the old-boy network— Silicon Valley companies took computer science majors to nice restaurants and entered them in raffle contests for iPads.

In the past few years, tech companies added room in their hiring budgets for college dropouts, such as former *Wired* editor-in-chief Chris Anderson's 3D Robotics. As tech start-ups turned from small businesses into corporations—some nearly the size of Wall Street investment banks—they had to hire engineers quickly. Silicon Valley has always favored the young, since they are more likely to stay abreast of the newest computer science programs, but now, having to hire a lot of people for expanding companies, tech giants were seeking the self-taught. It turned out that many tech CEOs preferred someone who had learned autodidactically rather than from a professor at an Ivy League school. The first issue was that technology was improving faster than educators could teach it.

Pinterest was just one of the companies trying to find talent before institutions held it captive. Whenever Quixey cofounder and chief science officer Liron Shapira wanted to convince his summer interns not to go back to college in the fall, he took them to a regular event he hosts called the All-Meat Lunch for College

Avoiders, acronymed AMLCA. At the Espetus Churrascaria in San Mateo, Shapira provided unlimited meat to any college-age job seekers who had decided to do one of the following: not go to college, drop out of college, or delay college by a year. He first posted the challenge on his blog in June 2012, asking, "Go to college or eat unlimited meat?"

"Think of someone you know who just graduated from college," he asked in the post. "Chances are, they're still hunting hopelessly for an 'entry-level' job. Well, you know what would make their job search a lot easier, and land them a job that's much better than entry-level? Taking four years of their life to build job skills." Shapira clarified that he didn't consider college worthless—just a bad way to spend four years of your life. "Espetus Churrascaria is a high-end Brazilian BBQ restaurant with great food, atmosphere, and service. They have an all-you-can-eat lunch with seven types of steak," he said. "So ask yourself, do you want to go to college, or eat unlimited meat?"

Since then, Shapira had hosted about a half dozen lunches at Espetus. Shapira himself dropped out of UC Berkeley after interning at Slide, a company that created third-party apps for Facebook that sold to Google. He ended up finishing the degree eventually, but "I just did it for the social signaling," he said. "I didn't do anything too heroic, and I'm largely a hypocrite. At the time, I had no alternative." He would tell Quixey interns that he was advising them not to go to college only because they were extremely talented—"three or four standard deviations from the mean of the bell curve." Otherwise, going to college for the average person was a rational decision.

The lunches, he said, "don't change a lot of minds, but help people realize college shouldn't be the default option." Most people who attended, he said, were already considering doing something like taking a year off or starting something new, and the conversations they had with Shapira nudged them toward that decision. What Shapira, a Thiel fellow mentor, was trying to prevent was "status quo bias": the idea that the human mind assumes the status quo is the best option. "If you're extraordinary," he reiterated, "then don't count on college to set up your life's challenges."

Shapira said the problem was that when you're seventeen, you think of yourself as a child who has to tread along through a system. "What if you thought of yourself as an adult, and you just have to go on with your life?" he posed. He would tell young people that instead of following the track they think they should be on, to look at senior positions they're interested in and start learning the skills that will get them there.

He thought the idea of applying for entry-level jobs was ridiculous. Instead, he told young people to think of their ultimate goal first. Climbing corporate rungs was so ten years ago. "Looking for an entry-level position is a sign that you haven't planned your life," said Shapira. But that is the period of time, around eighteen years old, he said, that job seekers had three years of leeway to train for whatever it is that they wanted to do. "If you acted like that at eighteen, you'd spend your time wisely, versus if you were in college, you'd spend your life different—wasting your time until you were twenty-two," he said. "College gives you nothing that can help you with your life aside from this piece of paper that will make your job search slightly less hopeless."

Shapira thought that watching classes on YouTube or Khan Academy, an online education platform, was just as good as going to college—and possibly more effective. "There's a simple way to go to your computer and learn more efficiently than in any classroom," he said. "I think we're seeing the beginning of a revolution."

The Thiel fellows had already begun thinking this way, but for many of them, going from a structured school system to fending for themselves in Silicon Valley was daunting. Some of them joined the area's incubators, which, in a typical Silicon Valley accelerated pace, had become a sort of West Coast Ivy League. In Silicon Valley, education was based on your proximity to start-up incubator or to a Silicon Valley god. Who do you learn from? What corporation do you work with? To what circles can you pin your education? Here respect came from the extended networks you knew.

At incubators, instead of learning old code from older professors, participants can meet like-minded young techies on the cutting edge of computer programming. With incubators such as Y Combinator, Techstars, and 500 Startups becoming more relevant signaling mechanisms to the tech industry than an Ivy League degree, many teens think that getting into an incubator is more likely to give undergrads the skills they need to get a job in an increasingly tech-focused economy than a handful of humanities courses in a liberal arts college. Plus, the incubators were becoming more and more selective, and producing tangible results—like the billions the Dropbox and Airbnb founders made. Whereas college degrees used to provide students with insurance that they would have a credential to fall back on, graduates were finding that the more reliable safety net was the ability to program. In the second Silicon Valley boom period of 2010 to 2015, employers couldn't find enough candidates to fill their job openings, and as undergrads increasingly couldn't find jobs, the only people who could fill the chasm were those with computer science skills. The fast track to get them all together: an incubator.

Each of these incubators was shorter than the Thiel Fellowship and somewhat more structured. The meals and events were highly encouraged, and the leaders had office hours that students could book online. It was a more appealing format to some of the fellows, such as Burnham and Jonathan Marbach, who applied to Y Combinator online. Started in 2005 by angel investor Paul Graham, "YC," as it was called in the valley, accepted a smaller percentage of applicants than Harvard, Yale, or Princeton. Though it had no central headquarters, and was run from Mountain View, those admitted to the three-month program had access to a valuable network of Silicon Valley entrepreneurs and investors, possible cofounders, and a constant stream of high-powered speakers. At the end of every section was a "Demo Day" where participants presented their company ideas to investors.

By 2012, Y Combinator had launched over a billion dollars in business, hatching companies such as Dropbox, Airbnb, and Loopt, the latter a now-defunct location sharing service for mobile phones. Y Combinator has two classes, or cycles, each year, during which companies moved to the Bay Area for mentorship and programming partners. Both of the three-month cycles revolved around building new companies. And though there was no fixed YC home, participants met one another and possible mentors at weekly events where a different Silicon Valley god would come speak. The atmosphere of the weekly dinners recalled High Table, the Oxford University tradition where students meet with their professors for dinner once a week, but the vibe was decidedly Silicon Valley. Meals were on rolling white tables instead of long candlelit tables for twenty. Instead of black tie, the aspiring founders wore T-shirts and carried laptops to show off what they had coded over the course of the week.

Jonathan Marbach went through Y Combinator as soon as he finished his last semester at Wake Forest. He left college to do both YC and the Thiel Fellowship. His attendance there was the reason why the team split. He applied to YC from college. After he was accepted, he moved out to Silicon Valley on January 1, 2012. There he spent his days trying to come up with a new idea that would solve one of the world's problems. "The biggest thing we could think of was email overload," he recalled. "The direction we went was figuring out a way to automatically filter distracting emails that we want to see on our own time, leaving only important ideas in our in-box." The program's advisors worked with him and his partners to craft the idea, but by the end, it seemed that most people didn't want to switch over from Gmail, and they had few users.

Once YC ended, his new partners lost interest and moved on to other companies, breaking up the team. Marbach moved back to New York to be closer to his family. "In Silicon Valley, I wasn't very closely connected to anyone," he lamented. "It was tough to coordinate anything." Without a car, being so far from the other fellows made it difficult to keep up with them. In retrospect, YC was the best part of Marbach's fellowship. He said the partners in it were company founders themselves, and he found Graham more accessible than Peter Thiel was. "I could meet with him whenever I want if I just submitted a form," he said. "He even emailed me out of the blue saying, 'Hey, John, how's it going?'

"I don't know if he actually cares, but that actual action matters a lot."

After the dinners, each guest speaker talked about the start-up he or she built and how it got to where it was, before a question-and-answer session with the audience. The rest of the week, nine full-time YC advisors, all entrepreneurs and investors, counseled the start-ups during "office hours": Paul Buchheit, Aaron Iba, Carolynn Levy, Jessica Livingston, Kirsty Nathoo, Geoff Ralston, Harj Taggar, Garry Tan, and founder Paul Graham.

Born in 1964, Graham gained notoriety for founding Viaweb, which later became Yahoo Store. Since then, he worked as a computer programmer and venture capitalist before starting YC. Other partners who also have equity from the YC companies are entrepreneurs Sam Altman, now the head of the organization; Justin Kan; and Emmett Shear. On-staff lawyers offered YC founders advice for free.

Companies had a support network to figure out problems, come up with ideas, and help those who were stuck figure out what to tackle. The advisors would tell YC participants they needed to figure out what users would want and then ask themselves to name their own strengths. Usually by the end of the program, 15 percent had iterated on their original idea so much that they had a different plan from their original one. Once they figured out their idea, the advisors instructed the founders on where to start and how to do it quickly, and how to get users as fast as possible, in order to figure out whether what they were building was promising or a dead end.

Graham thought that weeding out a bad idea was where Y Combinator could be most valuable. On his site, he wrote about how identifying bad ideas could produce good results: "Paradoxically, these disasters are precisely the reason to launch fast: they all represent problems you're going to need to solve eventually, and the only way even to find out what they are is to launch. In practice, they vary from technological bottlenecks to threats of lawsuits, but the most common problem is that users don't like the product enough."

When the start-ups were ready, the founders would go to the advisors during office hours to get help on how to launch their product, and how to show it to users, the media, and investors, usually starting with a website. After they had completed this step, they worked on the pitch process by sitting with YC partners in front of whiteboards and figuring out what story to tell and to which news outlet to give it. Then came fund-raising. YC partners advised on how much money they should raise and from whom, when to raise it, and what their financial goals should be. More money was not always better. "If you try to climb too steeply, you just stall," said Graham. "Similarly, if you try to raise too much for the stage you're at, you'll not only waste lots of time and end up with nothing to show for it, you'll even jeopardize your chances of raising a smaller amount, because your initial leads will cool as you start to seem shelf-worn."

By the end of the cycle, the companies got ready for Demo

Day by practicing presentations, filming them, and rehearsing in front of the advisors and partners. Midway through the cycle, partners from Sequoia, one of the area's top venture capital firms, came in to talk with each company team. By acting as consultants, Sequoia got an early look at the start-ups, and the start-ups received early feedback.

Along with dinners was a party for founders at the beginning and the end of their three-month time, as well as regular happy hours in Palo Alto and Mountain View bars. Founders organized their own social events too: a Herculean task for engineers who enjoyed coding over keg stands. Often YC "batches" would become each other's cliques going forward. Through its founders and alumni, YC's connections alone were reason enough to stay in the Bay Area. They also provided access to reporters, who in turn helped the companies raise their profiles so they could in turn raise money.

The first Demo Day in 2005 attracted fifteen investors. Fast-forward to fall 2012, and four hundred investors showed up to see what company ideas come out of the program. By 2015, there were over five hundred. Afterward, contacts are made and follow-up meetings scheduled. Though the program ended that day, YC stayed in touch with the new start-ups through their negotiating period, and sometimes negotiated with the investors themselves. Y Combinator has become its own signaling system.

Other start-ups that came through the program enabled

their founders to exit with hefty nine-figure paychecks, including Cloudkick, Heroku, and perhaps most prominently, Reddit, whose cofounder Alexis Ohanian acts as the East Coast ambassador for the program.

Like Thiel, Graham encouraged founders to launch on the West Coast rather than the East. "The Bay Area is for start-ups what LA is for the film industry," he contended. "Large numbers of the people you meet by chance have some connection to it." And while he didn't rail against college in the same way as Thiel, Graham said, "Y Combinator takes only three months—less than any school—and afterward start-ups can go wherever they want."

For all of YC's popularity, however, a story about the incubator's marginal success ratio posted on Graham's blog in fall 2012 surprised both investors and entrepreneurs alike. He admitted that all YC companies' returns are concentrated in just a few big winners. Also, he wrote, "The best ideas initially look like bad ideas." It turned out that while the total value of the companies he had funded with Y Combinator was $10 billion, three-quarters of that amount came from just two: Dropbox and Airbnb. A generous estimate would be that only one company per "batch" would have a real effect on YC's returns. Therefore, he said, each participant's chance of success didn't matter nearly as much as his or her chance of succeeding in a huge way. And that chance was tiny. "The probability that any group will succeed really big is microscopically small, but the probability that those nineteen-year-olds will [achieve exceptional success] might be higher than that of the other, safer group," Graham said in the post. "The first time Peter Thiel spoke at YC, he drew a Venn diagram that illustrates the situation perfectly. He drew two intersecting circles, one labeled 'Seems like a bad idea' and the other 'Is a good idea.'"

For example, investors were largely skeptical of Airbnb at its inception. Graham couldn't convince anyone else to fund them. Out of his entire venture capital network, only Greg McAdoo, a venture capitalist at Sequoia who had worked in the vacation rental business, gave Airbnb a chance. As of fall 2012, the company was valued at $2.5 billion. Three years later, it was valued around $25 billion.

"The intersection [of a bad and good idea] is the sweet spot for start-ups," wrote Graham. Finding that sweet spot, though, is a problem that almost cancels itself out. "The vast majority of ideas that seem bad are bad," he went on. "When you pick a big winner, you won't know it for two years."

The one metric that Y Combinator could track is how much each new start-up can fund-raise after Demo Day. But that's the most misleading number of all. "There's no correlation between the percentage of start-ups that raise money and the metric that does matter financially, whether that batch of start-ups contains a big winner or not," he said, adding, "except an inverse one." Even if most are bound for failure, however, the experience the entrepreneurs get among one another working on ideas they care about was likely more real-world experience than they'd get in an East Coast institution, and more ownership than they would on a traditional career path. The best part for many of them was that there was always a backup plan: they could go back to doing what everyone else did—college—*but* having already started a company. In a world where failure was a virtue, it didn't matter if the venture closed in three weeks and never made a cent. At least they went out and tried.

Techstars, the incubator behind the eponymous *TechStars* reality show on Bloomberg TV, started in 2006 in the unlikely city of Denver by an entrepreneur named David Cohen. Its pace was faster than YC's, more public and more akin to a tech start-up reality series. A career angel investor, Cohen had already founded three of his own companies in Colorado, including Pinpoint Technologies, a medical company, and the music service earFeeder.com, before he realized that he'd rather invest. So he decided to build a network with which to do so.

Cohen wanted to see how new companies would do as part of a network for three-month periods, much like Y Combinator, and then decide whether to keep them as part of his portfolio. Cohen's first step was assembling a group of mentors, and he eventually built a network of seventy venture capitalists, CEOs, and entrepreneurs who would mentor the new companies they hoped to test.

The first program launched in 2007 with ten companies. By fall 2016, five from the first program had been acquired. Two years later, Techstars launched in Boston, and the following year in Seattle. In 2011 Techstars NYC launched in New York, directed by David Tisch, then the thirty-year-old scion of wealthy Daniel Tisch. At the time, it was a controversial choice to have a nonentrepreneur billionaire's son direct what was supposed to be a scrappy group of tech founders. With the New York branch, the group launched a "Global Accelerator Network" to programs in twenty-two different countries together with President Obama's Startup America Partnership.

They then launched the *TechStars* reality show, the first attempt at start-up-related TV before Bravo's *Silicon Valley*. This Bloomberg series followed the batch of 2011 companies based in New York. Episodes were supposed to offer glimpses into the lives of the entrepreneurs, complete with the start-up lingo of "whiteboarding" and "pivoting." One, Jason Baptiste, cofounder of Onswipe, compared the start-up life to war on the show: "Physically it's not like war," he said, "but mentally it's the exact same thing." Though the other mentors and founders in the program found him "arrogant," they couldn't help but be impressed with his company's growth. It turned out they had a point. When he defended his attitude on the final episode, he said, "You have to be confident—you have people whose lives depend on this."

Throughout the first series, the Techstars founders raised $25 million. While some did better than others, they all preferred their newfound careers to what they were doing before—or at least they said so on the show. For example, Melanie Moore, cofounder of ToVieFor, an online handbag store where customers could choose the price they wanted to pay, used to work in investment banking. She would find herself and her team stuck late at the office night after late night. Though ToVieFor is now defunct, starting a fashion business was much more fun and more dramatic.

Furthermore, it didn't hurt that founders got to fraternize with mentors featured in the show, such as Foursquare executive chairman and cofounder Dennis Crowley, Tumblr CEO David Karp, HubSpot cofounder Dharmesh Shah, and Fred Wilson of Union Square Ventures. Now Techstars has programs in Seattle, Boston, and Boulder, Colorado, among other US and international locations. Each city had anywhere from fifty to one hundred mentors for the ten to fifteen companies that go through the program each year.

Like the other incubators, Techstars boasted a lower acceptance rate than Harvard's: just 1 percent. "We have selection rates lower than the Ivy League, so you have to be among the best of the best to earn investment from Techstars," its website advertised.

It would also claim that the three-month program was more rigorous than four years in college. Along with working out of Techstars's office space, the chosen companies got to present in front of investors in their network. They received $20,000 up front in exchange for 6 percent of common stock in the company they created. Techstars counts that initial $20,000 as $200,000, since it offered an optional $100,000 convertible promissory note. Like YC, Techstars, too, had dinners where speakers prominent in the tech world would come twice or three times a week. Founders also visit companies in the area to meet CEOs and entrepreneurs there.

During the first month of each program, the founders presented their ideas to mentors and received feedback so they knew whether or not they would have to "pivot," or change direction. The next month, they ironed out specific issues and ways to expand or develop certain products. The third month, participants figured out what to do after the program, such as how to fundraise and pitch investors, and eventually launch their company. The culmination of the program was, again, a Demo Day, where outside investors and entrepreneurs could come see the presentations of the final companies.

Some of these companies worked out well. SendGrid, a cloud email platform, generated over $60 million in revenue in 2015 and is projecting $100 million in revenue in 2017. Graphic.ly, a digital comic book site, raised $7 million by 2014. AOL, Jive Software, and Automattic acquired companies the first year too.

They said their start-ups averaged raising over $2 million in out-side capital. To apply, Techstars also had aspiring founders fill out online applications. They could apply with tech ideas in software, Web, social media, consumer Internet, but not biotech, restau-rants, or "local service-oriented companies"—areas in which the Techstars founders and mentors had little expertise. Applicants could already be making money and have funding, or they could be starting out cold. But "nothing is too early," they said.

Then there was 500 Startups, which worked more like a venture capital firm but on the angel level. The smallest of the better-known incubators, it was the brainchild of entrepreneur and angel investor Dave McClure, a former tech consultant to Microsoft and Intel, and later director of marketing at PayPal. When he left PayPal in 2004, McClure started investing in con-sumer Internet start-ups such as Mint (acquired by Intuit), Slide-Share, Twilio, Credit Karma, Wildfire Interactive, TeachStreet, MyGengo, Mashery, and Simply Hired, among many others. He eventually became investment director for Facebook fbFund for about six months before running FF Angel, a seed-stage invest-ments program at Peter Thiel's Founders Fund. The fund seeded early-stage start-ups that were developing apps for Facebook.

At least ten 500 Startups companies have been acquired, and its second fund raised another $50 million in outside capital. McClure also started expanding into the New York market, into media, fashion, and entertainment. Still, 500 Startups has not had the same success as Y Combinator, a fact McClure was well aware of and posted about extensively. "YC is quite clearly the Yankees, while 500 is more like the Oakland A's," he wrote on his blog. YC, he said, backed the "billionaire start-up club" of companies such as Dropbox and Airbnb, whereas 500 Startups's largest exit was MakerBot, which sold to Stratasys for $403 million in June 2013. "YC is for hackers, and 500 is for hustlers," McClure quoted his cofounder as saying. "YC is unbeatable in engineering and programming culture, and 500 is best in show at marketing, design, and story-telling culture. They are chess nerds, and we are band geeks. YC made fire. 500 stole it."

McClure thought that seed round valuations for decent companies at $3 million to $7 million were a good pace of growth for founders and investors alike, and had "more sustainable pricing." Still, he praised YC as "the Giant whose shoulders we all stand upon, 500 and others included." He wrote, "They are kicking everyone's ass, and they are easily King of the Hill."

Along with incubators came newfangled universities aimed at replacing traditional institutions. There was venture capitalist Tim Draper's new Draper University of Heroes. Though far smaller in both size and reputation than YC or even 500 Startups, Draper, lately best known for his sizeable investment in Theranos, took an extra step to replace the university with the incubator by creating a for-profit incubator university. Best known for funding Skype and Hotmail in their early stages, Draper had long been a proponent of teaching students about business and entrepreneurship. But he had never gone as far as he did in 2011, when he decided to buy the Benjamin Franklin Hotel in downtown San Mateo for nearly $6 million to turn it into an entrepreneurship university. His plan was to host classes of students in a makeshift boarding school for ten-week academic programs geared toward entrepreneurial skills, based on Stanford's schedule.

The hotel would be a test space for Draper's pilot program, which was to open in winter 2013. "The pilot has gone viral, and there have been hundreds of applications submitted from all over the world," Draper said in his initial announcement. "We clearly are going to need to hire some more admissions people well before we open in January." Though the community originally was critical of Draper's proposal, complaints were about the parking rather than the alternative education. Draper reassured neighbors that students wouldn't be allowed to bring their cars with them.

Draper University opened in April 2013 with 41 students. They lived on the first three floors. Classes took place in a lobby lounge. Eventually it hopes to host 150 students. The slogan? "The world needs more heroes." On the school site, there was no president; instead, Draper was "the Riskmaster."

"We are building divergers who want to be better and do better," read the early mission statement. No matter that *divergers* wasn't even a word—grammar wasn't the focus here. "Expect to be inspired. To do things you didn't think were possible. To be fearless." Each student would create his own company and build a network of mentors and coaches, just like at the incubators. In the end, just as at the accelerators, they would pitch Silicon Valley investors for funding. The curriculum was "centered around superhero themes"—invitations to the opening night informational had a background of Marvel-looking superhero cartoons—and students could participate in activities such as "public speaking, cold calling, hydroponics, yoga, car racing, riflery, future projection exercises, speed reading, and business simulations." And rather than investing like at typical incubators, Draper charged students $9,000 to $15,000, depending on the length of the session.

It was just the first step toward what was already happening on the East Coast. There, universities from Harvard to Northeastern had started building their own versions of YC, albeit with Ivy League professors and classes. It turned out there has been such a flurry of start-up activity in recent years that now one in three business incubators were housed on campus, up from one in five in 2006. Even Duke and Syracuse Universities—better known for creating star sports teams than spawning start-ups—are planning incubator spaces. Thanks in part to Thiel and YC's Graham, the experiment to expand Silicon Valley had begun. The question was whether campus culture could keep up.

6

Alpha Girls and Beta Boys

Nearly a year into her Thiel Fellowship, in spring 2012 Laura Deming was having little luck raising money for her fledgling Longevity Fund. She hadn't gone back to school, but she had returned to a college campus to work out of a Stanford lab testing mice to figure out ways to make them live longer. The lab turned her onto new talent. There she looked for promising young scientists and companies that her longevity venture firm could invest in. It gave her solace to be near Stanford, even if she wasn't technically a student.

Deming enjoyed living among the other fellows in Palo

Alto, but she hadn't quite figured out how to come up with new concepts in the lab and meet potential donors who would invest in her fund—and at the same time source new biotechnologies to extend human life. Then there was her social life to worry about. It was all rather overwhelming. She decided to become a fruitarian.

In her longevity research circles, she was used to meeting scientists who were always tweaking their diets to see how they would feel. Laura came across people practicing calorie restriction as well as more typical diets of limiting carbs or fat. Some of her tech friends saw their bodies as machines, constantly adding and taking away food groups to test productivity differences. One had tried eating only fruit. So to raise her energy, she swore off all meat, bread, and dairy for the sixth months of her fund-raising efforts. Her dainty body became an even fainter wisp, and she slept less and less each night. But her focus and clarity increased, and she found she could get much more done during the day. Deming also found that her new diet fit in with a strange social landscape that was proving different from the one she was vaguely aware of at MIT, where she had started working in a lab at age fourteen. At MIT, she was comfortable among the scientists in their spectacles and white lab coats. The research assistants found her somewhat of a curiosity. Here was a tiny little prodigy passionate about testing the life-spans of mice.

But in Silicon Valley, everyone was some version of a tiny

little prodigy. And they all acted like their bodies were nuanced machines in need of a special treatment, which included an enlightened diet, fitness regimen, or mating system to make it run better and code faster. Being a fruitarian helped her fit into a place where baseline nerdiness wasn't nearly enough. You had to be weird in some specifically difficult way that made you more productive at the same time.

Deming fit that bill. So did Noor Siddiqui, at least for John Burnham. Noor applied to be a 2012 Thiel fellow, the year after Burnham, in secret. She didn't want to tell her parents, or anyone else for that matter. Her mother and father, both born in Pakistan, had moved to the United States to get a better education. They hoped their children would have the same opportunity. They moved to Washington, DC, where they studied at George Washington University. They wanted Noor to go not only to college but also to graduate school. She tried bringing up the fellowship when she read about it online, but they opposed it and told her not to apply.

Her father in particular thought teenagers should be in school. They wouldn't know what to do with $100,000 and at that age couldn't know what their lives would be like. But Siddiqui had an idea of what she wanted to do. Having been to Pakistan, she saw what poverty in that part of the world is like—and then saw the comparative advantages in the West. She wanted to find a way to connect poor people in the East to wealthy employers. The idea appealed to the Thiel Fellowship organizers who chose Siddiqui to be a finalist.

She was so enthusiastic about it that her parents consented. "Once she's through with the fellowship, it will allow her to go wherever she wants," her father said. Still, he wasn't happy about the way she'd be living, which was even more socially lax than he thought college would be. He didn't like how close she'd be living and working with boys. Noor had considered living at TheGlint, with some other Thiel fellows, but he disapproved.*

During the fellowship, she would be mentored by previous fellows, which was how she met Burnham. He offered to help her navigate the program. Soon the two were dating. But there was little time for socializing. Siddiqui was supposed to be working on her idea. She did this mostly from home in Virginia, in a room she called "the cave." She covered it with pages torn from magazines and inspirational quotes from Abraham Lincoln, Paulo Coelho, George Bernard Shaw, and Coco Chanel.†

Her relationship with Burnham helped the transition, but she tried to keep it secret. She soon learned that she was lucky to have found someone among the group. Few really dated one another. Even Deming was growing frustrated with the dearth of

---

* "Jumping off the College Track," by Jessica Goldstein, *Washington Post*, August 3, 2012.
† Ibid.

eligible gentlemen, despite all the attention she got, as well as the ostensibly favorable 10:1 male-to-female ratio.

Deming soon realized that being female in Silicon Valley was different than it was on the East Coast. The conversations women had with one another and with men were different to start—as were the clothes they wore and the social circles they aspired to join. In Palo Alto, few girls wore heels or dresses or skirts. And walking down University Avenue, you'd be hard pressed to find a single lingerie shop. Most ready-to-wear clothes were for camping. Wrap or shawl? Forget it. Polar fleeces were for throwing on when the sun went down.

She found that walking through Mountain View, Sunnyvale, or Palo Alto in a dress was akin to getting ready for the prom at noon—or it would label a woman as an East Coast visitor or maybe a costume party guest. Jeans were the uniform for both sexes. Men did better if they wore Steve Jobs's favorite kind of sneakers to prove that they had something in common with the tech master—whose legacy lived on in his stock price and user interface.

Women's jeans could be loose or tight, but pants were essential. For women, proving that you were not a slave to stereotypes of sexuality was essential. The more that brand logos were replaced with company logos, the better. Instead of flaunting Coach, Gucci, or Polo brands—big no-nos—any logo or slogan should refer to a start-up (even start-ups that were, by their bank accounts, bigger than the brands they were replacing, such as Facebook, Google, and Apple). The earlier the T-shirt was made in the company's history, the better—2005 was almost nascent, for example—since that would signify how much equity you might have and how wealthy you could indirectly say you were. Wearing a Facebook T-shirt made in 2007 was a stronger symbol than driving a Ferrari, since a Ferrari costs about $200,000, while an early-stage employee at Facebook in 2007 could have made tens of millions of dollars after the IPO.

Instead of attractive athletes or suave businessmen, the most desirable men in Silicon Valley for women looking at that kind of thing were numbers five, six, and seven employees at big tech companies. Standing on line at University Café one day, a girl nearby pointed to a pudgy redhead and squealed, "He was number five!"

Women don't wear the nautical look or the drapery dressing of an East Coast resort town. Sailboat dresses or anchor patterns would signal Virgin America commuter. The less cutesy, feminine, and frilly you could be as a Silicon Valley woman, the better. Of course, all women like to feel attractive, which you are allowed to do, as long as it is mostly through toning, rather than an expensive dress. Skirts are okay as long as they have pockets, similar to jeans, or somehow resemble construction-type attire, showing one's toughness. "Someone told me I was dressing like an idiot, because I had basically gotten a bunch of teenagerish dresses from college and was parading around in them without thinking about how I looked," she remembered. "The advice was basically to look more professional—lose any short skirts and start wearing blazers and stuff." She thought she followed it for the most part, but instead of blazers she wore combat boots—and definitely kept the miniskirts. Anything delicate or lacy or detailed showed weakness.

San Francisco is a little bit different. Though Twitter and the mobile payment company Square had taken over the Mission District, remnants of an older world remained. San Francisco attire is more nuanced. With a more even sex ratio and more opportunities for socialization, as well as the San Francisco society holdouts acting as a foil for the new tech set, the transgression and disruption there often take the form of costume parties—at least on the fringes.

By the height of the second tech boom, from around 2010 to 2015, tech companies such as Facebook and Alibaba had hundred-billion-dollar IPOs, San Francisco society was finding itself in a strange position. Its members used to chair the museums and opera houses, but now they couldn't donate nearly as much as the tech CEOs. In fact, they couldn't even keep their old institutions afloat. They had to befriend those techie couples to keep the board humming. At the same time, the techies were willing to fraternize with the old guard for validation. Back in their parents' garages, they'd never dreamed of chairing the museum ball or running the hospital benefit. But now they had made it.

There may have been vestiges of an appreciation of gender differences in San Francisco, but down on the peninsula, it was a different story. There androgynous dress extended to mating behavior. Men were too busy coding to be men. When they were really working—in "flow"—coming up with a program, racing against the clock to build something before the next person took their idea, their physicality basically was irrelevant. They acted nothing like the testosterone-fueled bankers on the East Coast. Their feet were planted. Their sexual rage didn't come out in boozy pool parties but on late-night online "dates," if they were lucky. Silicon Valley was a sexual wasteland, many coders found at first.

While Deming wasn't opposed to the favorable ratio—she said she never felt out of place being the only woman at a party, or in her house, even where many of the male fellows became her good friends—she soon realized that many women around her were angry about the lopsided gender ratio in Silicon Valley, which has been counted as 60 percent male and 40 percent female, but felt a lot more male heavy. The women complained that men were "beta," while women were "alphas"—especially those who followed Facebook COO Sheryl Sandberg's *Lean In* cause, the movement inspired by her bestselling book that encouraged women to lean in and take control of their careers.

Sandberg, however, dressed like a Washington bureaucrat, which many thought she aspired to be. It led other women to feel that they should act like they could play with the boys and not have to dress like they wanted to attract them. Deming didn't particularly look up to Sandberg. She admired scientists and philosophers more. But in Silicon Valley, she found that women commonly mated with younger men because of the social demographics. The young men were the wealthy ones, having grown up working as early-stage employees at big tech companies. Single women preyed upon them at places like the Rosewood Hotel.

Many of those who were married didn't talk about their husbands much. They didn't want to be the "wife of." Successful women in Silicon Valley wanted to be known as such in their own right. One of these women, Aileen Lee, was among the relatively few female venture capitalists Deming had heard about. She was intrigued by Lee's new fund, Cowboy Ventures.

Lee had been living in the area for over a decade and was part of the inner cabal of Silicon Valley women. "I'm obviously thinking a lot about gender," she acknowledged, sitting outside on the deck behind the Rosewood. "People are racially sensitive and disability sensitive, but they're just not gender sensitive. I mean the Tinder situation?"

She was talking about Whitney Wolfe, the cofounder of Tinder, who had recently left the company to start Bumble, a competing dating app. Then there was Ellen Pao, the KPCB partner who had charged the venture firm with harassment. Pao said she was routinely passed over in favor of male partners, excluded from all-male company ski trips, and subjected to harassment from a male partner, but her suit failed, and she had to pay her former employer more than $200,000 in legal fees. She ended up opening a conversation about gender equality in Silicon Valley. On top of those scandals was Evan Spiegel, whose emails were leaked to Valleywag.

Lee left to start her own firm, Cowboy Ventures, in 2012. Its mission would be to seed early-stage companies that improve daily life through technology. Leaning in over the lounge table between us, she said she found herself tougher on women, because she thought they needed to be tougher in this world.

"There is an attitude that is, 'Boys will be boys,' and there's no societal consequences," Lee was saying. She thought the public should boycott companies that treated women badly, the same way people boycotted South African companies during apartheid.

Lee argued that women were responsible for much of the online purchasing on the Internet. They drove the success of many successful e-commerce companies. They played more social and casual games online than men. She saw them as responsible for the success of many tech companies. In a widely shared article on TechCrunch, she posted that female users drove most traffic and made many companies successful—a feat for which they weren't properly recognized:

If you are already targeting female customers, have great women working in your company, and are seeing strong commerce and social network effects, congratulations. You are likely trying to figure out how to handle hypergrowth right now. Plus, your office probably smells pretty good. Women are the routers and amplifiers of the social web. And they are the rocket fuel of ecommerce. The ongoing debate about women in tech has been missing a key insight. If you figure out how to harness the power of female customers, you can rock the world.

Two years later, though, she thought Silicon Valley had made some improvements in its attitude toward gender. In part because of the dustup over Pao, Lee thinks companies are now more sensitive to gender. "The number of women in venture capital has actually decreased in the past decade," she said in fall 2016, "but the awareness and sensitivity has hopefully improved in the past five years," she added. "If you look at tech companies, they are starting to report their diversity numbers publicly. We're very far as an industry from being a reflection of our country and from reflecting the college graduate population, however."

To make up for it, it seemed, boys would be boys, and girls would be boys. Husbands' last names were often not taken, and girls stuck together. They graduated to queen tech bees such as Sandberg.

In the same circle as Lee was Andreessen's wife, Laura Arrillaga-Andreessen. She too still lived near and worked on Stanford property. Her father had developed the land around Silicon Valley. Even though she and Andreessen together were worth billions, Arrillaga's tastes were in keeping with other success stories of her ilk. For example, she didn't hesitate to advertise her preference for Taster's Choice coffee.

She didn't brag about expensive tastes and played down any signs of wealth. The only thing that she, and many Silicon Valley people, advertised was busyness. Braggadocio included comments about not having any time and being overly enthusiastic about nonleisure activities, such as one's job. Arrillaga-Andreessen had been a philanthropy professor at Stanford for nearly twenty years but had recently launched an online course and a giving website. "I think this whole convergence of philanthropy and technology is so exciting I can't stand it, and it's the reason I never seem to be sleeping and always seem to be drinking Taster's Choice and yelling when I talk," she said.

Arrillaga-Andreessen, forty-six, was the first person to teach philanthropy at the Stanford Graduate School of Business when she joined the faculty in 2000. In 2014, she started the Laura Arrillaga-Andreessen Foundation, an organization that she said operates as a philanthropic innovation lab. It aims to democratize giving by providing online resources and programs to make donating more accessible to people at all levels of wealth. As her field increasingly moved online, so did she: in fall 2014 she released her massive open online course and made the six-week online program in collaboration with Stanford free to all.

For now, Arrillaga-Andreessen was trying to figure out more ways to encourage people to donate, working seven days a week on philanthropy. She kept a disciplined schedule, waking up at seven in the morning to have breakfast and exercise, and then working from eighty thirty until seven in the evening before breaking for dinner with her husband—usually a microwaved meal in plastic Costco TV trays, she said. Then they worked for another three hours together "side by side." Afterward, she would read a book for one of her three book clubs. She also lightened her day with daily dance parties at her foundation's office. "One of the great parts of running an organization," she said, "is mandating that we all dance once a day."

Arrillaga-Andreessen knew Thiel and was familiar with the fellowship. Deming was impressed by what she had achieved—and by what was possible in the valley. She liked the women's lives she heard about.

These people she met there, weirdos for sure, existed to break every rule and disrupt every institution: automotive, with electric cars and sharing apps; marriage, with swapping wives and husbands; and politics, with pervasive libertarianism. Here she could do whatever she wanted, she thought. And if her fund took off, even live forever.

7

The Immortals

L aura Deming was about to present to the 2015 Forbes Women's Summit, but she couldn't decide whether or not to mention one of her most radical ideas for human life extension. She knew it sounded extreme and kind of crazy. Should she just settle with "Avoid sugar," the pat advice she knew was the one proven thing you could do without the help of drugs? But there was this other idea too.

She had learned that when the gonads were cut off worms, they lived 60 percent longer. "I can't really tell people to take out their ovaries," she said sheepishly. But she was torn. Evidence really did suggest that eliminating reproductive potential seems to increase life-span in worms and in people and possibly in mice. "Korean eunuchs live a quarter longer than their contemporaries," she said. The reasoning? She guessed that having nonworking sex organs would make an animal's body think they were just temporarily not working and therefore would "have to hang around longer" to have time to reproduce. Or, she thought, because animals spend so much energy in pursuit of reproduction, maybe not having that need would let cells relax a bit. Whatever the case, Deming found it fascinating.

It wasn't just the science that fascinated her but also the idea that such a long-held belief—that everybody dies—could be wrong. She didn't expect to find the answer during her lifetime, but she didn't consider it out of the realm of possibility. Deming had wanted to "cure" aging since she was eight years old. Home-schooled by her parents in New Zealand, she was encouraged to teach herself math. She remembered her father telling her how beautiful math could be, describing the "intricate spiraling numerical patterns," and how they "could—and did—save the world on a daily basis." "How we were a walking, talking summation of billions of tiny biological calculators, each calculator a cell, and each cell a miniature cosmos in its own right," she explained.

John Deming, a former investor, painted for her a colorful picture of science's heroes, such as Archimedes, Galileo, and

Nikola Tesla. "I couldn't believe they were all dead, and that I would never get to meet them and hear them talk," she recalled.

However, there was one legendary living scientist to whom she could talk. Deming had long followed the work of Cynthia Kenyon, an MIT biologist. Kenyon had been working on ways to extend human health and life—and it seemed like she was making progress. She had doubled the life-span of a roundworm by disabling a single gene.

So when Deming was eleven, she wrote to Dr. Kenyon to see if she could meet her. A year later, Deming went to see the famed scientist when she was at the University of California in San Francisco, whose faculty Kenyon had joined in 1986. Kenyon asked her if she wanted to work in her lab. Laura was thrilled she'd be able to perform real experiments. Her family moved with her from New Zealand to California so that Deming, at age twelve, could take Kenyon up on the opportunity.

"I got to fiddle with lasers, scoop up mounds of microscopic worms, and stare mesmerized as the modified, glowing creatures writhed and wriggled around a plate," Deming remembered. She learned how to decode scientific papers and look for proteins and pathways. "I got to feel the elation that comes when you discover something nobody else has seen or known, the satisfaction of clicking in the final puzzle piece," she said.

At UCSF, Deming was an anomaly. After all, she was twelve. She sat in on lectures and met professors and lab students who helped her get through an advanced course load. But still, she wanted to go to MIT to study biology as an official college student. At UCSF she had self-structured her curriculum with a collection of online MIT lectures to supplement what she was doing at UCSF.

By the following year, at age fourteen, she had matriculated to MIT as a freshman biology major. She still felt a bit out of place. She worked with mentors at the Weiss Lab for Synthetic Biology, where she learned about quantum mechanics and advanced biology, and eventually decided to look for a way to extend human life.

Deming applied for a Thiel Fellowship with the idea to extend human life. She wanted to encourage and fund new ways to study how to do that. When Laura gave her presentation back in 2011, there was one audience member who was particularly intrigued by her. Aubrey de Grey, whom Thiel had funded, wanted to help her.

De Grey entered Thiel's world a few years before, in 2007. Dressed in ripped jeans, a denim shirt mostly covered by his foot-long beard and long, greying hair, the professor was sitting on the windowsill in his cramped New York hotel room facing a drab inner atrium. He was disappointed. He had just flown over from Cambridge University, where he is based, to appear on ABC-TV's *Good Morning America*, but the show's producers had canceled last minute because they feared he was "apparently too technical for their dumb audience," as he put it. De Grey had just written a book called *Ending Aging: The Rejuvenation Breakthroughs That Could Reverse Human Aging in Our Lifetime*, in which he put forth his theory of longevity: basically, there were seven reasons why we age, and if we got rid of each one by one, then we could cure aging. It would be easier to cure than cancer, he thought. And since we've developed cures for so many kinds of cancers, we couldn't be that far from an aging panacea.

For the past twenty years, de Grey had been researching how to reduce cellular degeneration through mitochondrial mutations and free radical pollution, both of which contribute to aging and disease. Stroking his beard, he described the three "bridges" in his program. "Now all you can do is keep healthy through exercise and longevity therapies. In bridge two, we'll have gene therapy." He was already studying how to take genes out of the body and combine or replace them with other genes before injecting them back into the bloodstream. Today new genes were often rejected because they were inserted directly into the body, so the immune system kicked in when it detected a foreign body and destroyed it. And the third bridge, he said, was nanotechnology, in which cell-sized robots would be engineered to enter through the bloodstream to fight off diseases.

But that was all a ways away. At the moment, he was focused on funding—from Silicon Valley. There they were more open to his sometimes zany-sounding ideas. "It's a bit edgy, a bit contro-versial," he admitted. One problem was that people wanted to invest in a closer exit strategy, and this was more of a long-term possible payoff. "Another problem is that these guys worry they're going to be laughed off the golf course," said de Grey, adding with a smile, "There's a herd mentality even among billionaires." A major coup was getting a $3.5 million donation from Thiel to research extending human life-spans by curing aging. "Rapid advances in biological science foretell of a treasure trove of dis-coveries in this century, including dramatically improved health and longevity for all," Thiel said at the time. "I'm backing Dr. de Grey because I believe that his revolutionary approach to aging research will accelerate this process, allowing many people alive today to enjoy radically longer and healthier lives."

It took Thiel a year to decide whether or not to fund de Grey, ultimately making the decision in 2007 because, as de Grey put it, "I was sufficiently out of the box so I wouldn't be swayed by academia, but I had the right credentials being at Cambridge and so on." The professor said that Thiel had been instrumental in in-troducing him to investors in San Francisco. "Peter is a visionary," he said, "and San Francisco is the epicenter of the visionary bil-lionaire demographic." In San Francisco, de Grey hired an event planner named Allison Taguchi to organize dinner parties and speaking engagements to fund-raise for his research.

De Grey thought the power of his persuasion hinged on

proof of concept, which he planned on demonstrating through "robust mouse rejuvenation," which would be funded by the billion dollars he hoped to raise. For mouse rejuvenation to work, he would need five hundred scientists studying a strain of long-living mice (three years), wait until they were aged two, and then try to extend their lives until their fifth "birthday" using SENS tactics such as stem cell therapy, gene therapy, and nanotechnology. "If this is achieved," he posited, "the scientific community would be convinced."

De Grey himself was convinced already. While he conceded that there was nothing that could be done at the moment to extend life, "as long as you don't smoke or get fat," he hoped the robust mice will prove that the longer you live, the more likely you'll be alive when his treatments are available for humans. De Grey compared the human body to a car. "If you maintain an old car, it will work indefinitely," he said. It's a concept high-level CEOs can understand: according to de Gray, Amazon honcho Jeff Bezos had expressed interest in his work, as had erstwhile junk bond king Michael Milken, a survivor of prostate cancer who founded the Prostate Cancer Foundation.

By the time Deming was involved in longevity efforts, the drive to live forever, or at least exponentially longer, was a popular topic in Silicon Valley. Just like hacking other problems, Silicon Valley entrepreneurs wanted to solve the problem of death. There were a variety of methods already being tested, such as being frozen at Alcor Life Extension Foundation, like Todd Huffman of Langton Labs was planning to do.

It wasn't a new strategy after all. For decades, billionaires such as Howard Hughes and Edward O. Thorp, author of the 1962 bestseller *Beat the Dealer: A Winning Strategy for the Game of Twenty-One*, had been hoping to live forever.

Back in 2007, around the same time that Dr. Aubrey de Grey was making his tech world fund-raising push, Edward Thorp was sitting in his spacious Newport Beach, California, office opening up his translucent orange bottle of pills when his cell phone rang. "Give me your name and number!" he demanded, and then snapped, "I can guarantee you I'm never going to buy a Honda!"—in the process spilling about twenty horse pills and even more tiny white ones all over his desk.

Upon hanging up, he bent over to sweep up the stray medication, picked up one, and asked, "Want to try one?" Thorp was talking about the bigger pills, a cocktail combination of "life extension" drugs that he'd ordered from the Life Extension Foundation in Fort Lauderdale, Florida. He procured copies of its brochure, newsletter, and order form from their prominent position in a stack on the windowsill looking out to a sunny day above a nearby mall. Inside were articles on recent studies about the longevity benefits of common nutritional supplements such as omega-3, resveratrol (found in red wine), and grape-seed extract, and some not so typical, including velvet deer antler, optimized cat's claw, and shark cartilage. There were also ads for the inaugural Life Extension Cruise in Miami aboard the Norwegian Sun. Inside Thorp's pill bottle, though, were only the company's life extension mix of pills and baby aspirin, "to reduce inflammation."

In recent years, the computer science pioneer had become increasingly focused on his own longevity. While his supplement and exercise regimen had kept him at least ten years younger, with smooth, tan skin and a balmy grin, Thorp wasn't leaving his future up to medicine. He was a member of Alcor, a foundation that practices cryonics. Thorp did not plan on dying but freezing—or vitrifying, rather—for the next few hundred years, or at least until someone came up with the technology to "reanimate" him.

It all started when he read a book called *The Prospect of Immortality*, first published in 1962 by a science fiction writer named Robert Ettinger, about coming back to life after freezing. Ettinger went on to start his own cryonics institute that still exists today in Chicago. "It all made sense to me as a possibility," Thorp said, squinting as he made a gagging expression (he had swallowed a longevity lozenge). As he looked around for one of the suitably named Glacia mints he has on hand in case he has trouble swallowing, he explained how he found someplace to have cryopreservation done himself. Cryonics International, the company founded by Ettinger, was low cost, at $28,000 a head, but the Alcor Life Extension Foundation, the country's largest cryonics lab, was the facility he settled on. He was impressed that Hall of Famer Ted Williams, the Boston Red Sox baseball legend, had entrusted the lab with his body to freeze upon his death at age eighty-three in 2002. "I once saw him play in Boston toward the end of his life," Thorp said nostalgically, still sucking on his Glacia mint. "I could see that he was different from anyone else out there. Maybe I'll see him bat again one day."

While Williams elected to have only his head frozen, Alcor offered the possibility of having one's entire body frozen, for $120,000. The organization, based in Scottsdale, Arizona, was started in 1972 as the Alcor Society for Solid State Hypothermia, as a nonprofit in California. In 1967 Alcor performed its first cryopreservation (staff members still wince at the word *freeze*, since their technology, they explain, does not technically freeze people but "suspends," or vitrifies, them in temperatures below minus 120 degrees), and by 1990, membership had grown to three hundred. A few years later, Alcor relocated to Arizona. Apparently the risk of earthquakes in California was too high, but Thorp said it had more to do with red tape regarding the rights of the cryopatients. Now, with more than eight hundred members still living—and seventy-six cryopreserved in large silver thermoses, known officially as "Bigfoot" dewar containers— Thorp believed it was an institution "that would be around for a while." This was an important consideration, since he planned on being suspended there for two hundred to three hundred years. He went with the whole-body option, because while others trusted that bodies could eventually be cloned from the DNA in your brain, "there's more memory in your whole body than your brain. It would be weird to adjust to a new body," he said.

Alcor's strategy rested on the concept that the body didn't die immediately upon "legal death." The idea was that in the first ten minutes after cardiac arrest, the brain was still warm and working, and there would be little damage to the bodily organs. That's when Alcor's suspension team would rush in and begin rapid cooling and transportation to an Alcor thermos. Todd Huffman had instructions tattooed on his body describing how to do it. The sooner they could get there, the better, from a preservation standpoint.

So when Thorp felt he was nearing his deathbed, he would notify Alcor's suspension squad to be on standby should he perish. They recommended, however, that members relocate to cooperative hospice facilities in Scottsdale. In any case, Alcor personnel would wait for Thorp during this critical near-death time twenty-four hours a day. When his heart stopped, they would race in (assuming he would be at a hospital that allowed cryopreservationists to intervene) and place him in an ice water bath before restoring his circulation and breathing artificially with a heart-lung resuscitator known as a Lucas chest compression device, or cardiopulmonary support "thumper." Then they would hook up his corpse to an intravenous line and administer free radical inhibitors, anticoagulants, pH buffers, anesthetic, and other drugs to maintain blood pressure. Once his temperature dropped to a few degrees above water's freezing point, they would drain out Thorp's blood and replace it with an "organ preservation solution," or cryopreservant, since blood has a tendency to crystallize at low temperatures.

"It's like chicken," said Thorp, swirling around in his chair with jackknife-straight posture. "If there are ice crystals, it doesn't taste the same as if it were never frozen." The old technology at Alcor was to freeze patients, which would break cell walls. Now the outfit had a solution that maintained the structure better. "The old line was you can't turn a hamburger back to a cow. Now it's not a hamburger anymore," explained Thorp. This transfer of blood out and cryopreservant in could take hours, which was why Alcor recommended being close to the facility. After this "cryoprotective perfusion," Thorp would be cooled by nitrogen gas fans to prevent ice formation. Then, over the next two weeks, he would be cooled further to minus 196 degrees. (The lowest temperature ever recorded on earth was minus 129 degrees in Antarctica in 1983.) At this point, he could be lowered into the dewar full of liquid nitrogen, where he would remain at that temperature for the next few centuries—or however long it would take a new generation of Alcor employees to figure out how to wake him up again.

Thorp had thought a lot about what would happen when

he was eventually reanimated. He had put away a multimillion-dollar trust (he won't say how much, but has previously put the number at $50 million) that would collect interest over the years and fund the science required to turn him back on. He was less concerned with the physical part than with the psychological aspects of reawakening in the future—since he figured that by then, he would just be able to go to a blood bank to get new blood, and scientists would be able to clone whatever body parts had suffered wear and tear from the many years of being inside a thermos.

"Who knows what the world will be like then," he wondered aloud. "You could wake up, and the language could be different." Shaking his head, he added, "But none of these things are very likely. I just always think of extreme cases, since that's paid off for me in the investment world." While Thorp put his chances of coming back at only 5 percent, that's up from 2 percent a few years ago, when he learned about new research in nanotechnology. Plus, he had recruited family and friends to join him for the long haul. "It would be nice to have a group of people going through the same thing," he said.

Deming was skeptical of Alcor's ability to extend life. "The question is, I'd be a lot more afraid of the integrity of the business surviving than the science," she said. However, Laura thought there was proof that freezing some parts of the body could actually work, explaining, "Some portion of you is preservative." She believed that coming back to life after being frozen was unlikely but "not infeasible." What she found less likely was that the business would still be around after any of us was living, let alone the thawed corpses. "That to me is way more disconcerting than the whole science part."

This reasoning motivated others in Silicon Valley, such as Thiel and Google's Larry Page and Sergey Brin. They, along with Sean Parker and executives from Facebook, eBay, and Netscape, were pouring millions into biomedical research, much of it aimed at living a lot longer. Google even hired futurist Ray Kurzweil to become a director of engineering. There he works on enhancing human capability through technology. He believes he will live forever.

Some viewed the body as similar to an advanced piece of computer machinery that could be reprogrammed and enhanced. Just as computers had improved, so could biotech, and biomedical research. The nanobot revolution could be right on the horizon. Gene therapy and reprogramming the neocortex were just a couple of the other ways that life extension could happen. Buying a lottery ticket, maybe. But if you won, the payoff was far greater than money. They already had cash.

As Deming was trying to raise money for her Longevity Fund, the field was getting more crowded. In 2013 Larry Page started Calico Labs, devoted to antiaging research. A year later, Calico recruited Deming's mentor Cynthia Kenyon to leave UCSF and join him. Google invested up to $750 million in the company billed as a health venture start-up aimed at "curing" death. The goal was to coax life-extending abilities out of animals.

Deming was still in touch with her early mentor, but was looking at smaller companies she could have more influence on. Still interested in the science herself, the young woman worked in the lab a few days a week and was fascinated by how the genome could be realigned. It was hard to explain those interests to investors, though. "The big problem with biology is there's no way to logically talk about things," she said.

Fund-raising was slow going. "Starting a fund is really, really, really hard," she said. "It's so much harder than I thought it was going to be. You have to convince very skeptical people to give you their capital to invest." It was a real hard sell in her case because the results were so far away. She said she spent two years just figuring out how to talk to people.

There was the problem of explaining to prospective investors what the companies did. One company made simple modifications to drugs that would enable new versions of it to be easily approved and used. Another company was involved with gene editing, which meant cutting the genome in a specific place and inserting new genetic material. It was still far from commercially accessible, however, since before, putting the gene in the wrong place could possibly cause cancer, or worse. But with this technology, the gene editing was so targeted that it could be safely used.

Deming was working with advisors to figure out which version would be the best bet. Her days consisted of meeting founders, trying to find companies, and then asking her investors whether they'd want to invest. At the same time, she had to translate their work into lay terms.

Deming wasn't sure if her backers were as excited about biology as she was. Most people just wanted to hear about a magic pill to live longer. So that's what she started working on.

Two existing drugs, metformin, prescribed to manage type-2 diabetes, and the immunosuppressant rapamycin had proven to have the side effect of extending the life of mice. She thought these pills could be refocused on longevity, if only they could minimize or eliminate the rather unpleasant side effects such as chronic nausea, shakiness, and dizziness. A distilled version could provide this magic pill everyone was looking for. It could potentially become available to the public within ten years and possibly cure aging. A pill, she thought, would eventually make people live an extra twenty to thirty years, and at age sixty or seventy, it could make people feel thirty.

In summer 2015, the FDA approved a trial to look into the antiaging possibilities of metformin. Over five years, the medication would be studied to see if it had the same effect on humans as it did on mice. It would be given to three thousand elderly people who were already at risk for life-threatening diseases.

She and other scientists didn't know yet whether the drug

would merely make people older for longer—posing problems to the health care system, the job market, and the pension system—or would make them healthier for longer. Scientists were trying to make sure they were extending "health-spans," not just life-spans. Maybe aging didn't have to mean declining health. Maybe it could mean extending health, and maybe that could happen through a pill.

Ideally, one of these pills would mimic calorie restriction, a proven way to increase the life-spans of animals, at least. But there were other ways to stay young. Deming was investigating a company that said it could delete old cells from the body. Scientists there were testing it in mice. They also injected older mice with young mice's blood, which Laura conceded sounded kind of gory, but it worked.

One of her advisors was Dr. Joon Yun of the private equity firm Palo Alto Investors, where he worked as a venture capitalist investing in health care companies. He too became intrigued and decided to start a biology prize similar to Russian investor Yuri Milner's Breakthrough Prize, offering an enterprising scientist $1 million to "hack the code of life" to uncover even more possibilities for delaying the aging process. Like Craig Venter, the geneticist who first sequenced the human genome in 2003, and Peter Diamandis, the entrepreneur who started the XPrize, his focus had turned to extending life-spans. Dr. Yun didn't see a limit to human age.

Larry Ellison, the billionaire founder of Oracle, also supported antiaging research, and was trying to find ways to at least extend the health-span, if not live forever. Google, meanwhile, was working on "ingestible tech": a capsule full of iron-oxide nanoparticles that would enter the bloodstream and identify cancer tumor cells for early detection of many kinds of cancers. Another company, Proteus Digital Health, was developing a sensor pill that would send information it uncovered in the body to a person's smartphone. And Diamandis's foundation was working on a device that could discover indicators for diabetes, tuberculosis, and abnormal blood pressure, all with a drop of blood that could be taken at home.*

Deming had joined a community of bigwigs whose new focus had become the same as hers. She found herself being asked to speak on panels throughout the valley. She was awarded prizes left and right, mostly because she knew something about the science—and had a handle on this magic pill that so many people wanted so desperately.

---

* "Silicon Valley Is Trying to Make Humans Immortal—and Finding Some Success," by Betsy Isaacson, *Newsweek*, March 3, 2015.

8

Five Minutes of Fame

Laura Deming had become the darling of Silicon Valley's aspiring immortals. Her seeming proximity to this magic pill was a pull so strong that unlike the other dozen or so fellows who had quietly gone back to college (three her year), or given up their ideas, her presence was expanding.

"Too Young to Fail" read the headline of the MIT *Technology Review*'s story about her a year into her Thiel Fellowship. But on the inside, Laura wasn't so sure it was true. The way the press had covered her, it was like she had already succeeded, but she still felt she had little to show for it. Article after article, in the *New York Times* and the *MIT Technology Review*, called her a prodigy. The young woman was styled, groomed, interviewed, and featured. She was asked to speak at conferences alongside experts in the field; after all, she was a shock to behold. Next to a panel of white-haired scientists wearing lab coats, here was this gorgeous, passionate vixen—an oxymoron in a biologist's body.

"The cool thing about Silicon Valley is that, though people might be skeptical of youth, they don't actually know that you're not smart enough or capable enough to make it work," she told *Technology Review*. At least she had confidence in her scientific intelligence, if not her business acumen. It was an odd sensation, though, riding the wave of publicity but scrambling to keep afloat at the same time. As she scoured the tech news, reading about billion-dollar company valuations, one after the other, she wondered whether the same thing was happening in those larger cases. Theranos, the biotech company that promised to inexpensively perform dozens of blood tests with a pinprick instead of a vial, was worth billions—but the device turned out not to work as claimed. Whereas Deming tried to court biotech investors, she noticed that Theranos had attracted investors with little scientific background. They had previously invested in enterprise and social media tech companies. Was that how no one realized Theranos's real abilities, or lack thereof?

What did these valuations mean? It seemed like much of the publicity in Silicon Valley was generated by a handful of operators. They were part of the networking machine of which she was becoming aware. Out in the valley, where newsprint newspapers were practically an anachronism, news came through blogs and tech platforms such as TechCrunch, and lately the Information, a tech news site started by a former *Wall Street Journal* writer, Jessica Lessin. There was also Recode, a collaboration between Walt Mossberg and Kara Swisher. Tidbits were insidery, and these outfits often provided ways to meet as well.

The yearly TechCrunch conference was where Thiel had made his original announcement to convince students to drop out of college. Run by an entrepreneur named Michael Arrington, TechCrunch had become more than just news. It was a database for company founders to post information about their businesses. It had become a status marker, listing valuations, partnerships, and funding rounds. Then there were PandoDaily and the Hacker News, written by insiders for insiders, often about engineering issues. Many of these revolved around who to hire. Good product designers were hard to come by, and the big companies like Facebook, Google, and Apple had serious pay packages to offer.

There were the gossip sites such as Valleywag, for instance, that existed mostly to taunt wealthy executives. Valleywag outed

Thiel as gay in 2007. By January 2016, it had closed, in part thanks to a lawsuit filed by professional wrestler Hulk Hogan, and funded, to the world's surprise, by Thiel. Ever since Valleywag attacked him, Thiel had been out for Valleywag's parent company, Gawker Media. So when Hogan (Terry Bollea, in the real world), sued Gawker for posting a sex video of him with his friend's wife, Thiel anonymously contributed more than $10 million to the fight, leading legal experts and Gawker founder Nick Denton to wonder why Bollea refused to settle multiple times for amounts as high as $8 million and $10 million. In March a Florida jury awarded him a whopping $140 million in damages.

Finally, Andrew Ross Sorkin at the *New York Times* received a tip that it was Thiel who was the mysterious benefactor in the case against Denton. At the end of May 2016, Thiel admitted it, saying it wasn't revenge but just to deter Gawker from attacking others. A month later Gawker filed for bankruptcy, leading to a wave of fear that a billionaire with bad press could eradicate an entire media institution. Thiel argued that his case was a form of philanthropy, helping people persecuted by "terrorist organizations" like Gawker to defend themselves. He later wrote an op-ed in the *New York Times* titled "The Online Privacy Debate Won't End with Gawker," arguing for the passage of the Intimate Privacy Protection Act, nicknamed the Gawker Bill, which would make it illegal for outlets to distribute intimate images. Still others considered Thiel a hero, standing up against a company that many in the media didn't even count as legitimate.

Until its abrupt demise, Valleywag salivated over its characters' trials, twists and turns. Its writers went wild on the news that former Kleiner Perkins partner Ellen Pao was suing the firm, tearing into Kleiner's leadership.

The media outfits in Silicon Valley that stuck around longer were more "collaborative" with tech companies, such as Tech-Crunch, which took part in the start-up economy. Arrington considered his website a start-up as well, not a separate estate covering the industry, as many East Coast–based media outlets were.

Lessin, of the Information, also thought of her site as a start-up. She had married Sam Lessin, the founder of the file sharing company Drop.io, and moved to San Francisco with him. In the Bay Area she realized there was an absence of real media. Granted, all the major outlets had bureaus there, but there was no real technology-focused authority aside from TechCrunch, which many of the major venture capital firms worked with directly. So she started a subscription service for in-depth tech news called the Information, which costs $400 a year. To Lessin, a niche audience would be attracted to these kinds of deep investigations.

Still, the media world out there was different from what it

was on the East Coast, where she'd covered tech since graduating from Harvard in 2005. Out in the valley, there were no media hangouts or circles of reporters. Many reporters just hung out at the Battery, a new social club in downtown San Francisco that was the closest thing the city had to a private club, like the British import Soho House in Manhattan's Meatpacking District. At the Battery, journalists mingled with venture capitalists in an artfully exclusive members-only atmosphere.

The Battery opened in late 2013 with fanfare. An art installation featuring San Francisco–based artists gave the space an effortful edge. A neon sign doubling as an art installation read: "Hogwarts meets Victoria's Secret meets Guantánamo Bay meets Lilith Fair meets the DMV." The lofty ceilings and animal heads on the walls coupled with bright pieces of contemporary art looked as though they were built for a warehouse party in Berlin. But the people there didn't seem effortlessly hip or chic like one might imagine at a private club; they looked like they'd never left their dorm rooms. Still, the space, in a former marble-cutting factory, was a new kind of Silicon Valley chic: geek chic. There was the twenty-person hot tub, the five bars, the secret cigar rooms, and a sprawling penthouse suite.

Founded by two entrepreneurs, a husband and wife named Michael and Xochi Birch, who started the social networking site Bebo, the club was based on London's social clubs. The Birches sold their company to AOL in 2008 for $850 million and then bought it back five years later for $1 million.*

Building a London-style club in San Francisco was a risky experiment. They didn't want only tech people, but somehow it seemed as if everyone camped out there was involved in tech or covering tech. It was the home away from home; a fancier Starbucks with massaged kale instead of Mocchachinos. On a recent visit, the club was filled with venture capitalists and tech reporters. Parties were hosted by media outlets or culture organizations such as the San Francisco Film Society and the *Financial Times*. It was all manufactured buzz.

In San Francisco, manufacturing buzz was the new media. It seemed so easy, after all. You could just "hack media" like you could hack anything else. Facebook had started it, allowing each person to manufacture his or her own buzz, all day, anytime, in essence writing their own personal profile that they could update eternally and embellish. Much of this effort was left to certain queen bees of buzz manufacturing. Some women were considered doyennes of Silicon Valley's skeletal social scene. It was much like the buzzing of the Hollywood publicists shepherding actors and actresses in and out of interviews, but these women were more than that. They helped the Silicon Valley geeks socialize. They made matches and conjoined founders to

---

*"At a Bay Area Club, Exclusivity Is Tested," by Sheila Marikar, *New York Times*, January 10, 2014.

investors. In a place where social norms were anything but normal, publicists were as much facilitators, networkers, and strategists all at once.

One of these women was Marcy Simon. Petite, with long, bright blonde hair, tanned skin, and clothing showing off her curvy, toned figure, Marcy Simon grew up in New Jersey, far from the companies she now worked with. She started out in broadcast journalism and later made packaged video news for corporations and executives at companies such as Microsoft and Sony. She went on to consult for Microsoft, helping to launch products and the Bill & Melinda Gates Foundation from 1989 to around 2006.

She married a businessman and had three children, but when she divorced, she expanded her team to begin working more in Europe and Asia, starting with consulting for Alibaba in 2004. Through her network, Simon soon became known for getting people into prestigious events such as the World Economic Forum in Davos, Switzerland. In the mid-2000s, she worked for the World Economic Forum, helping the conference become digital.

She helped brand a series of other conferences, such as the Web Summit in Dublin, Ireland, and assisted with lining up moderators and panelists at design conferences such as DLD (Digital-Life Design) in Munich, Germany. The conference system served as a perfect go-between for Silicon Valley founders temporarily between companies or trying to publicize companies, so that they could relay their own news rather than depend on a reporter who would be unlikely to get their message straight.

She had been a guide to a host of Silicon Valley entrepreneurs looking for access, and counted people such as Hyperloop One chairman Shervin Pishevar, Facebook CEO Mark Zuckerberg, and Uber CEO Travis Kalanick as her friends. She was also friendly with "super-angel" Ronald "Ron" Conway, who she said introduced her to a number of successful entrepreneurs.

With her Twitter handles "@teflonblondie" and "@marcy," she used social media to help promote clients' companies and even lobby lawmakers on their behalf.

One of Simon's stomping grounds was South by Southwest Interactive, a place that had become the Sundance Film Festival of the start-up world, where established Silicon Valley executives seek out new companies, and new start-ups try to go big. The official conference is at the Hilton in downtown Austin, Texas, but all the action takes place in the lobby of the city's two best hotels: the Four Seasons and the Driskill. One year, in 2012, Simon was holding court at the downstairs bar of the Four Seasons, which had turned into a heat map of Hollywood and Silicon Valley.

All around was engineering royalty, divided into two camps:

the nerd clan and the frat clan. The nerd clan embraced their intrinsic nerdiness, nerding out with thick-rimmed glasses and loose T-shirts emblazoned with obscure coding references covering an either skinny or portly physique. The frat clan were the nerds who worked out.

There were so many Silicon names at South by Southwest that attending the rest of the festival was almost unnecessary for the upper echelon of visitors. Simon was arranging for Apple executives to meet with developers as Steve Bing walked through the lobby with his staff. Lady Gaga's former manager Troy Carter was getting ready to host an afternoon hackathon. Nearby were Justin Bieber's manager Scooter Braun, 500 Start-ups founder Dave McClure, and Josh Abramson, who launched the popular comedy website College-Humor. Simon was there with Celestine Johnson, who was representing Eric Schmidt's venture capital firm Innovation Endeavors, which had sponsored an "innovation mansion" where entrepreneurs running their twenty-two portfolio companies could stay for the week to brainstorm.

Marcy's eyes darted around the room to see who she could make introductions to—they were in the thick of SXSW deal making. "We're creating this playground, their dream environments for them to foster innovation, to cultivate community," Johnson was explaining. It was based on DevHouse, a Palo Alto company that housed engineers together to encourage them to come up with ideas. "I heard the founders of Pinterest actually met at a DevHouse," she confided.

Surrounding her in the lobby was a mash-up of tech company workers and Hollywood types, which was partly intentional. Agencies in Los Angeles had started to hire actors to partner with start-ups for promotional activities. Now the trend was to create viral campaigns matching celebrities with tech product launches. Uber, the ride-sharing app, got endorsements from such celebrities as Ashton Kutcher, Neil Patrick Harris, and Kate Upton.

As Uber's Travis Kalanick walked across the lobby, Simon flagged him down. Nearby, two former Apple executives on the couch were telling him his logo was too masculine. But Kalanick didn't want to give the *U* a curlicue to feminize the concept, so he told them he was sticking with his manly upside-down horseshoe. "Travis continues to be focused on leading the vision and direction of the company from the early days to the present," said Simon, who was an early-stage Uber investor.

Dressed in designer jeans, a beige polo shirt, and a cowboy hat, Kalanick belonged to the engineering frat clan. It was the second year that Uber had sponsored Uber pedicabs in Austin through UberEats. This year they would be delivering barbecue. The iPhone app had added cows to the map of cars, and as Kalanick explained, "If you're hungry, you push the cow, and boom, bring me barbecue!"

Between the Uber barbecue ("powered by Iron Works") and Uber's recently launched site—including Ubers from Last Night (a spinoff of the site Texts from Last Night, on which people post embarrassing texts while riding Ubers the night before)—the company was making inroads. A few years later, it had expanded internationally. Uber's problem wasn't publicity but policy. Although Simon didn't officially advise Uber, her PR strategy helped other companies with that too.

She used to advise the Founders Fund, but more recently the firm was working with a different kind of strategist. Susan Mac-Tavish Best was the anti-Simon. Instead of flying around the globe to different events, she hosted get-togethers in both of her homes. Best looked Bohemian. Her ancestry was Scottish, and she still decorated her house with tartans. A self-described lifestyle guru, Best hosted parties for young founders and invited media there to mingle. She would make specialty cocktails in mason jars with cute little labels and colorful chalkboard signs of what dinner would be. For Hampton Creek, a "food technology company" that engineered plant food substitutes for mayo and eggs, she invited her media friends and Silicon Valley friends, as well as former Grateful Dead lyricist John Perry Barlow, which gave it all a flavor of old-world hippy-dippy community. She cultivated the young fellows on both coasts with the promise of being included in something that might be viewed as cool. She was a connoisseur of indie bands and start-ups on the verge that she would merge with reporters, venture capitalists, and entrepreneurs to give a little edge to a largely edgeless industry.

Her anti–Silicon Valley upbringing gave her a kind of carte blanche to be hoodie free. She wore dresses with plunging necklines, bright-red lipstick, and tight leather pants. In addition to Founders Fund, Best used to work with Lulu, a print-on-demand book publishing company, and Klout, a site that ranked people's social media presences. Lately, however, she had become the queen of impromptu techie feasts. At the same time, along with aiding in tech companies' growth, fundraising, and marketing strategies, she launched her own company, Living MacTavish. In San Francisco she hosted an evening on California's proposed secession with Tim Draper and novelist Michelle Richmond. On another night, she cooked dinner for Burning Man cofounder Larry Harvey and musician Jerry Harrison. Over the past year, she has held events featuring an interview with food writer Michael Pollan and artist Amanda Feilding on the use of psilocybin for end-of-life treatment for eighty and has hosted salons where entrepreneurs, distillers, and NASA engineers discuss what it would be like to live on Mars. MacTavish regularly runs sixty to seventy miles a week, so she interviewed *4-Hour Workweek* author Tim Ferriss and ultramarathoner Dean Karnazes on "going to extremes" in front of another crowd.

On the East Coast, she would do the same kind of networking

with entertainment people. But there, at least the media group she gathered had realized something: they felt the tug of technology, and it was taking their industry away from them. Technology had run away from the media and outrun it. The blogosphere, social media networks, and Twitter were replacing print, but they were so vast they couldn't be manipulated. Betting on people or betting on followers was not a meritocracy anymore. It was who had the most technological traction, and who had manufactured the most buzz.

Laura Deming certainly had buzz attached to her name, but it gave her an uneasy feeling. She was uncomfortable with promoting herself. She had heard that some people go to such lengths as manipulating Wikipedia pages. People posed as Wikipedia writers to change entries, but they were actually just publicists. Who needed facts? The blogosphere could run away with the news, the gossip could overwhelm the conversation, and even the subjects realized they couldn't control what was said about them. It was an irony that both Simon and Best, and now even Deming, were all too aware of. There was a huge disconnect between what the press knew and said and what the reality was. It was the fog of where the actual value was and what some of these companies actually did. The new media thickened that fog. What were these valuations? What was all this money?

What could these digital armies do if they changed Google results or made connections or gained followers for marketing reasons? What was failure if no one could see it? Deming wondered if she really was too young to fail, and if anyone knew what failure even meant anymore.

9

The New New Money

Laura Deming's friend Paul Gu was one of the quieter room-mates in the house she shared with five other Thiel fellows in downtown Palo Alto. Back in 2012, when they all lived there together, none imagined that he would end up being the most successful in their 2011 class—at least by funding standards. Gu had received far less press than many of the other kids in the class, such as Dale Stephens and John Burnham. He started the fellowship drifting from idea to idea without coming up with anything that stuck. Six months in he had nothing to show for it.

But then Paul hit upon a concept that would become a new

way to deal with money. It sidestepped the banking system and provided something different. His company would be among the first in Silicon Valley to let people loan to other people. It took out the middle man, it ignored the institution. It was so Silicon Valley.

The son of Chinese immigrants who came to the United States to study at Arizona State University and give their son a better education, Gu showed academic promise early on. He went to Yale University, where he soon assimilated into dorm culture and style. Gu was tall and wiry, and dressed in the typical postdorm uniform of loose jeans and a sweatshirt or baggy T-shirt. He blended into the background. But he was a welcome presence and a calm observer who smiled a lot. And he was focused on what he was doing. Deming liked him. He was her kind of person, after all. There wasn't the usual Silicon Valley trendiness about him. He wasn't trying to be a billionaire just after landing at San Francisco International Airport—though he wouldn't have minded. But still, his attitude was refreshingly free of affectation.

Deming had met Gu during the finals rounds at the Hyatt but hadn't gotten to know him back then. He'd stayed close to David Luan and Daniel Friedman, the fellows who started a robotics company together and who applied at the same time while they were sophomores at Yale University. In fact, Gu was with Friedman in the school science lab when he found out he'd won the fellowship. The calls came in on their cell phones, in succession. "We pretty much jumped into the air to chest bump and promptly dropped our phones, with the Thiel Foundation still on the line," Gu remembered later.

After accepting the fellowship, he moved from New Haven to New York, where the twenty-year-old started trying to figure out what his start-up would be. It was easier to leave school and start in Manhattan, where he already had friends, and it was easy to get around. It was different from college, but he'd experienced two years of school, and New York was new and exciting. There was so much more to do there than up in New Haven; plus, Gu was familiar with the city from weekend trips in with his friends.

At Yale, he'd taken economics and computer science, spending his days building trading models and doing problem sets— skills he thought would lead him to a career in finance. He knew he didn't want to go into academia. He always thought he'd do something in business. Wall Street didn't appeal to him, though. He was more independent and longed to start something on his own. It was this impatience that in part led Paul to apply to the fellowship. He just wanted to work for himself. When the Thiel Fellowship came up, he thought he'd go for it. Why not? "It seemed like sort of an obviously good thing to apply for," he remembered. "I did that and luckily got it."

While he was enjoying his social life, staying in touch with his Yale friends and meeting entrepreneurs in New York through a shared work space he used, he was starting to get frustrated that he couldn't come up with a company that worked. He and the co-founders he casually collaborated with to start a local e-commerce site called 404Market were frustrated and unable to attract any attention, or customers. Still, he gave it six months, but by month four was starting to look around for another opportunity.

Gu had been thinking about problems he could solve through technology. That was beginning to become the standard refrain among aspiring entrepreneurs: find a problem to fix. Lately, founders had become so overzealous in this endeavor that problems were created that never existed, or problems were oversolved to the detriment of practicality, such as iPad menus at airports, which took live servers to explain to frustrated users. It took Gu six months of working in New York to develop some real problem that wasn't being attacked from all sides by twenty- and thirty-somethings salivating to stumble upon the next TaskRabbit—a company that lets you find strangers who will do small tasks via an app. But then Paul realized the biggest unsolved problem was all too obvious: he knew too many contemporaries who were broke.

Some of his friends weren't doing so well, either. Gu didn't have a credit history, and he had no home to borrow against. He wasn't sure what to do. What if people could loan him money directly? Maybe they could do it online or through an app. Maybe he didn't even have to go through a bank.

When his friends tried to get loans to pay off their student debts or start companies, they had little to go on. So Gu decided he would come up with a formula that would predict people's future salaries based on their college performance and thereby give people—not institutions—enough information and leverage to loan directly. In return, the investor would get a percentage of the person's future salary.

He had also met his future cofounders: two Google employees who were twenty years older than he was and thought this idea of his could become a real business. They had been thinking about the same issues young people had, but they already had jobs—good ones. One of them, David Girouard, was president of Google Enterprise, a line of business products such as Gmail for businesses, which was rebranded in 2014 as Google for Work. They were established in Silicon Valley. Gu considered him the perfect partner. Girouard had the experience, and Paul had the algorithm that would use metrics such as a GPA, the person's career goals, and past internships to predict future salaries. They would join forces to start a new company called Upstart and would fund mostly young people who couldn't get a line of credit or a loan. Seven other student entrepreneurs wanted to participate, and the beta-testing team was formed.*

Gu realized early on he needed to get to California to have a

---

*"Paul Gu Tackles the Issue of Student Loans with Upstart," by Britt Hysen, *Millennial Magazine*, April 13, 2015.

shot. He figured the place to start a business was Palo Alto, not New York, so he packed up his Tribeca apartment and flew across the country and moved in with a few of the other Thiel fellows.

In spring 2012 he and his new cofounders raised money within a few weeks to get started, thanks to their connections through the Thiel Fellowship. The Founders Fund invested too. They worked in office space reserved for incubating companies in Google Ventures and then Kleiner Perkins—right on Sand Hill Road. It was like they'd arrived. But they hadn't, really; they were merely where it was all happening. Upstart had an algorithm, but it needed to find a seamless way to make the company work that would benefit both investors and those seeking loans. "We sort of had this general concept of a problem in mind, but the solution was quite different than what we are building today," Paul said.

Socially, Gu missed New York. However, the move was easier because he was living with Deming and two other fellows, Darren Zhu and David Luan. He soon adopted their routine. He was having a better time than some of the other fellows and didn't feel quite as isolated. It helped to have a focus. And his company was starting to get traction now that it had a few established Silicon Valley executives on board. Moving out there only after he had a workable idea turned out to be more helpful than he could have imagined.

Many of the others had moved around from house to house or from one co-living community to another. They had run out of their stipends sooner than expected. Gu, on the other hand, was getting paid, thanks to that early funding. Soon that amount would increase. He was also trying to solve the same problem with which the Thiel Fellowship took issue: the burden of carrying student debt into a world that didn't treat them like their college counselors did.

That first year and a half, the group was trying to figure out an income share agreement in which young people would share a percentage of their future income with those who had loaned them money. The idea was for it to be different from the way a loan typically worked. But other companies were catching up to them. The idea clicked with a generation of students who no longer could rely on tracked careers, or traditional industries, to offer them jobs upon graduation. It has been estimated that by 2020, 50 percent of the United States' workforce will be freelance. Steady regular full-time jobs weren't as common anymore.

But getting it right continued to be a challenge. "We pretty soon realized that was not going to be mainstream market product because it was very complicated, and a lot of manual time spent explaining what this was and why people should want it," Gu explained. They built different models, but the product was too complicated, so the team decided to make Upstart more of a traditional loan company.

Gu met some of his early investors through the fellowship's extended network of fellows. He met them at Thiel fellow functions and meet-ups. It wasn't that he particularly enjoyed going to these events. He mostly socialized to network. The fellowship didn't have a structured meeting system, except occasional Friday gatherings at a casual Palo Alto restaurant. "It was really just everybody doing their own thing," he recalled. Sometimes more organized groups got together, but usually everyone fended for himself.

Paul, however, seemed to thrive in this unguided system. He liked that there wasn't a formal structure to success there. "I think the sort of traditional system is very linear in that you know what to do in order to succeed," he explained. "You'll most deterministically get to a certain level of success, and, basically, when you're trying to start a company, there's not really a textbook for what exactly you need to do. And even if you do the things that are the textbook, it doesn't guarantee success—because the textbook doesn't really exist." Gu enjoyed the added risk.

Meanwhile, his job was to assess risk in the same way that East Coast businesses and industries did. His whole company used success metrics, such as GPA, to predict future success. At Upstart, Gu focused on specific ways to do that. "It's not whether you can pay [back the loan]," he maintained. "It's a question of how important you see your obligation." He realized that people who were diligent in school and studied conscientiously tended to honor their commitments. It was a way to judge people through data. In a place where social skills were poor, to put it mildly, algorithms served as a more reliable predictor.*

* "Using Algorithms to Determine Character," by Quentin Hardy, *The New York Times*, July 26, 2015.

Gu went so far as to say the algorithm even judged a person's character. Indicators pointed to warnings that someone might not necessarily be reliable, such as if he or she had used prepaid wireless numbers—a possible warning sign that the person didn't have a steady paycheck.

So now Silicon Valley was even trying to crunch data and numbers to determine character. Perhaps this data could predict a person's morality, responsibility, and reliability. Maybe cloud-based personnel software could replace human perception, and help human resources departments predict when employees will quit, how they will perform, and how long someone will keep a job. It characterized managers as "rainmakers" or "terminators." Analyzing employees through key words, such as a Google search, was becoming more and more common as even something as ephemeral as character was becoming digitized.

In a way, it was similar to how the engineers and kids who were nerds in school broke down what it took to socialize as if it were an engineering problem. By knowing all the data, they could figure out social cues and how they should talk and interact. Dating and mingling were difficult for them; maybe an algorithm could fix it. Engineers studied networking with an obsessive compulsion, thinking they could hack that too.

In one sense, the digitization of character was a way to remain politically correct while still sticking to the facts. The data didn't lie, right? Instead of offending anyone with subjective descriptions, digital character judgments were objective. They had predicted crime, after all, with systems such as CompStat in New York, a computer statistics management tool introduced into the NYPD in the mid-1990s. No one had to say, "That's a seedy neighborhood composed of this race or that race." The data did it for them.

So, they figured, why couldn't an algorithm decide whether someone would be successful or not? In a way, their system went against the Silicon Valley ethos. All of life was somehow quantified and could be expanded exponentially. Rocketing into outer space, for example, or changing the financial world code wasn't that impossible if it was just a bunch of numbers. Data eliminated the emotion, the fear, the—very rational—sense of failure. Numbers were cold, trackable metrics. There was no writer's block; none of the namby-pamby roadblocks you encountered in the softer subjects.

Gu looked at the numbers and realized that most millennials used credit cards to pay for things. "About fifty percent of the population in America have credit card balances that roll over month to month," he said. But even after building up even minimal credit, banks were hesitant to issue loans, allowing users to refinance credit cards at lower rates. They knew the grads had a lot of debt—after all, they had paid a lot of money for college. At Yale, for instance, Gu's tuition was $60,000 a year for room and board.

He became one of the few people ever to drop out of the university with three years' worth of credits. Gu started seeing that decision, and many others in his life, in terms of Upstart metrics. For him, the Upstart methodology became his world view. "I've applied this way of thinking not just to work problems or school problems, but actually to how I think about my life," he said. "For example, every couple of months, I will do a review of myself—an analytical type of review. I write three to four pages of analysis just on where I see my strengths and weaknesses going, what things I've improved at, what things I haven't improved at. I create a plan to sort of improve these things. This same process I would use in thinking about solving a credit modeling problem, I think I should also use when thinking about improving myself as a person and as someone who can contribute in the world."

But while Upstart's intention was to help finance entrepreneurs, Gu didn't think it was worth starting a company just for the sake of becoming an entrepreneur. Becoming an entrepreneur to "change the world" had become not only a cliché but also an epidemic. "I think it's important to have a problem that you care deeply about and have a way of solving that you really want to work on," he reflected.

The company officially started in early 2012. Four months after Gu and David Girouard came up with the idea, they handed out their first envelopes to the first few young students who were borrowing money using Upstart. The funds totaled just over $200,000 and would be given out at a restaurant in the Mission District in San Francisco. The students had never met, but they all had different kinds of ideas, such as a music platform or a novel. The idea would be to allow the twenty-somethings to do what they wanted rather than have to take a job just to make money.

"We're counting on you," he told the students, *Business Insider* magazine reported. "Don't spend it all in one place. And do the right thing—make us proud."*

The idea was to connect students with wealthy investors who wanted to help them build their companies. By the time it launched, the idea had spread. Upstart joined a growing field of companies, such as Affirm, founded by PayPal cofounder Max Levchin, and Pave, that were changing the way that loans worked.

As more and more students decided to take an entrepreneurial route versus a traditional path, they were finding few ways to finance their activities. Upstart was an answer. They often had to get day jobs, giving them less time to work on their passions.

Girouard thought that along with crowdfunding for people, Upstart should offer mentorships to help college graduates pursue the same kinds of career paths that had attracted Gu. He didn't understand why companies would recruit and hire graduates to help them raise money, when the recent graduates hardly had any network to leverage anyway.

---

* "A Group of Investors Is Buying a Stake in the Next Generation of Geniuses," by Alison Griswold, *Business Insider,* Feb. 22, 2014.

Instead, Gu wanted students to be free to figure out what they wanted to do without the added pressure of earning a steady paycheck. He didn't want other students to feel the pressure his friends had to go into banking or a hedge fund just to be able to pay rent. He also thought that other kids would feel the way he did about being his own boss. To millennials, reporting to someone else didn't seem as much of a given as it was to previous generations. This way, with funding, someone starting out after school could immediately feel ownership, Paul thought, from raising money for his own venture. Part of the plan was giving investors percentages of the borrowers' income. The borrowers would have to pay only if they were making enough money to do so. Students would sign up with goals and achievements, list their credentials, and then say how much money they needed to raise.

Then Upstart's algorithm would determine how much of their future earnings they'd have to share to make it worthwhile for investors. Some college graduates were more promising than others. Upstart expected them to make more money, so they wouldn't have to give as much of their income. Investors could pay graduates in increments of $1,000 and the borrowers made payments on a monthly basis. The most a graduate could offer for the future was 7 percent, and they wouldn't have to pay during times when they were earning only $30,000 or less a year. Both Girouard and Gu thought this system was ideal for entrepreneurs. They could focus on their companies at the beginning stages even if they didn't have a steady paycheck. Backers would benefit if the "upstart" did well, but the upstart wouldn't lose too much if he or she didn't.

Borrowers were called "upstarts." Investors or those who loaned to them were called "backers." That way, Upstart treated people as their own start-ups versus cogs in a machine. It was like a crowdfunding site for innovative people. In its first few years, Upstart funded upstarts from a range of professions, from poets, to artists, to bank founders. They have been self-published authors and writers, or promising graduates who still had to pay off their student loans. It would be a risky bet on a novel or an art project. They would receive a contract for five to ten years; if their earnings were below a certain number, they wouldn't have to pay their backers anything. Investors had to be accredited with the US Securities and Exchange Commission (SEC), as well as either earn more than $200,000 a year or have a net worth of at least $1 million. They weren't allowed to dictate how upstarts used the money, but they could and were encouraged to mentor and support them. Upstart took a cut of the deal, such as 3 percent of what students made up front, and then 0.5 percent on investments.

It was selling a chance to follow a dream, as was the way in Silicon Valley. And it was taking something that could hardly be predicted and attempting to make it predictable and quantifiable, which was also very Silicon Valley. It was also an attempt to cross class lines. Someone from a low-income family with a great idea wouldn't need family funding if he wanted to go into the arts. He didn't have to try to work at Goldman Sachs. The founders thought of it as democratizing talent.

"It's actually going to have a big effect on the socioeconomic makeup of America if we're successful," said Oren Bass, cofounder of Pave. "It's a huge leveling of the playing field."

Originally, Upstart talked to Pave about what they were doing, but the two companies had different ideas of what would work. A few years later, they were pretty similar, which was part of the problem. Both used data from colleges, the Internal Revenue Service, and the US Bureau of Labor Statistics. Both had to sign some sort of confidentiality agreement, too.

Critics argued that they were too similar and that their predictive models favored people who already had more advantages, such as those who had gone to Ivy League schools and those who had received job offers from known firms.* There were a lot of aspiring upstarts with degrees from Stanford, Harvard, and the Wharton School of the University of Pennsylvania. The loans often worked out that way because investors chose whom to back based on their education and area of interest. In some ways, the system resembled typical job applications.

Gu explained that his model revealed that the highest early-career salaries came from people with degrees in computer science

---

* "A Group of Investors Is Buying a Stake in the Next Generation of Geniuses," by Alison Griswold, *Business Insider*, Feb. 22, 2014.

from MIT. Those with Princeton economics degrees had the most midcareer success. It wasn't all that surprising.

Girouard responded to critics by saying the results were simply how the country was made up socioeconomically. It wasn't Upstart's job to correct for class divisions. "That's kind of a systemic challenge that our country has," he said.

They started to find that some majors predictably still led to more successful career paths and steadier salaries—at the very companies the apps had been formed to guard against students having to join. In a way, Upstart reconfirmed the traditional order of things, but it was aimed at finding unusual people who didn't want to have to do that. Gu still said it was mainly just geared to give people a chance to try something new.

"Like anything else in life, if you're not as smart or talented, or as ambitious or as creative, you're probably not going to make it as far," said upstart Trina Spear, a Harvard Business School graduate. "If you don't work hard and get good grades, you might not get as good a job." She used Upstart to launch her own company. "There's always going to be people that are better than others and have more opportunities than others. That's just life."[*]

Back in 2012, hers was the fastest funded start-up. She raised $20,000 in exchange for 1 percent of her income for the next ten years. She used the money to pay off her business school loans

---

[*] "A Group of Investors Is Buying a Stake in the Next Generation of Geniuses," by Alison Griswold, *Business Insider,* Feb. 22, 2014.

and put them into her own medical apparel company, Figs, selling scrubs, lab coats, and so on. Three years later, it had yet to take off. She wasn't able to draw a salary and thus couldn't afford her yearly payments. Now she wasn't so sure Upstart was scalable. And there was a limited return on investment. No matter how successful a borrower was, the backer didn't make more than $150,000.

As of 2016, more than 1,200 backers had invested a total of more than $472 million in 36,000 upstarts. Silicon Valley's venture firms were betting that it would be profitable. KPCB, Google Ventures, and billionaire investor Mark Cuban, owner of the NBA Dallas Mavericks basketball team, were all supporting it. Partnerships were piling up. Upstart had other ideas, such as collaborating with credit card companies, car loan companies—anyone who wanted to help rate people's credit ability.

Still, some investors started to worry that Upstart was enabling entrepreneurs who had little real promise. Would it just allow anyone to throw himself or herself into any crazy idea without much accountability or proof of concept? The company tried to balance that impulse by funding people with varied interests, such as art or design. It tried to find students who didn't want to sell their souls to go into banking or consulting just to pay the rent.

The ultimate goal for these loan companies was to become as large as something like LendingTree, the online lending exchange. Technologically enhanced versions of lending companies had been taking off since the recession in 2008 and 2009. Lending was another way that Silicon Valley was trying to disrupt banking, or at least rewrite its rules. In 2015 Jamie Dimon, the head of JPMorgan Chase & Company, warned in an investor letter: "Silicon Valley is coming" for their business. Tech entrepreneurs—so young, anyway—were noticing that millennials didn't want to save money, raise money, or bank in the normal way. They shopped online. Companies such as Upstart were fueled in part by people's growing distrust of the banking industry, which in Silicon Valley felt a world away—an old world, at that.

Millennials didn't like institutions; they liked start-ups, and they liked freedom, and they liked leaving behind the East Coast. Everyone was looking for a new way, especially after the New York finance industry had taken such a hit. Could Silicon Valley be the solution?

10

When Do You Beg Forgiveness and When Do You Ask for Permission?

By the end of 2015, the Thiel Fellowship's latest leader, an entrepreneur named Jack Abraham (who had replaced Danielle Strachman), was starting to counsel the new fellows on what to do in the event that their companies came under government scrutiny. It was a new concern for start-ups in Silicon Valley. Until now, government oversight was over single issues and only really touched Google, Apple, and other behemoths. But companies such as Uber and Airbnb started to change that because their existence required government consent. They changed laws in cities and upset local unions. Their new structures not only influenced the government's attention to the tech industry, leading officials to shine a brighter spotlight out west, but also they were changing political policies.

For most of the Thiel fellows, government intervention was a faraway worry. Abraham didn't have any go-to lobbyists on call at the time, but he knew which investors had more political connections. The new executive director thought the general rule with the government was that it didn't care about a company unless it started hearing about it, and word traveled of what the newcomer was doing to disrupt the "incumbent." The incumbent was the entrenched interest that the tech industry's lobbyists tried to unseat in favor of their tech clients, such as hotel lobbies and taxi and limousine unions.

"They have to be successful enough to be actually causing pain to a stakeholder in the local economy," said Abraham. "It takes a while for the pain to be acute enough for those organizations to go to the government." He advised founders not to alert the government about their companies without absolutely needing to do so.

"The preference is to avoid government as much as possible, and if they're required to interact, have people on staff who know how lobbying works," Abraham explained. According to him, there were known venture capitalists in the valley who knew how to deal with the government.

Most of the government interruptions, he said, happened at a local level, so having an ally nearby was valuable. The federal government wasn't involved in the tech industry as much as city governments were, though it differed state by state. "You never want to be in a position in a company where there's one person who could say, 'No,' and then your company gets shut down," he said.

By early 2016, the Thiel fellow James Proud, who had started GigLocator, had raised over $30 million for his new invention, a sleep device designed for the bedroom called Sense. He started it after his fellowship ended. The twenty-four-year-old from South London didn't like to be associated with the other young people in his fellowship class because he didn't consider them nearly as successful as he was. In his mind, he had arrived; they hadn't. Before moving to the Mission District, he had a spacious office in young, hip Potrero Hill, a neighborhood on the San Francisco Bay filled with tech offices, smoothie stores, artisanal coffee makers, and make-your-own gelato shops. All along Seventeenth Street, where his office was, young tech workers in the dorm-chic jeans and saggy backpacks walked back and forth, hailing Ubers and buses and riding their bikes.

From the outside, Proud's office looked like it could be a greenhouse. Through the small, narrow front door, it seemed like a jungle with all the palm fronds. But upon opening the door, the space soon took on the familiar characteristics of a start-up: a hive of workers clacking away on their laptops, a snack area in back filled with products containing the au courant ingredients such as chia seeds, avocado flavoring, green-tea extract. The fridge full of cold-pressed coffee was placed in the front of the kitchen. Proud sat at one of the picnic benches near a lunch spread of quinoa, kale salad, and chicken whose vital juices looked like they had been steamed so far into oblivion all that was left was a block of protein—all the better to engineer with efficiently.

All was going so well that Proud was expanding into a bigger office. He wanted to hire more people and had already been doing so at a clip, flying to Norway, London, and Finland to recruit worthy engineers. He found a space nearby that nearly doubled the company's footprint and amped up its design: an old warehouse with exposed brick walls and glass-lined offices. Proud posted it to his Facebook page with a picture of his swelling staff. "Where are you in the photo?" asked one friend. "I'm the Annie Leibovitz," he replied.

Meanwhile, other health tracking companies were coming under the radar of the US Food and Drug Administration. A few, such as Fitbit, the fitness tracking device, were getting FDA scrutiny. They laid out the guidelines for "low-risk devices" and specified that it could not be advertised to cure insomnia or anything else, but only to promote general wellness. Devices of this nature, said the FDA, couldn't be a threat to customers' safety. Ad claims had to be as vague as possible. *Sleep management* was okay to suggest, but curing sleeplessness? Proud's company was one of many that had reached a certain size and could become a threat to the existing industry, therefore attracting the attention of the government regulators.

Heather Podesta was sitting in the lobby of the Sheraton New York Times Square Hotel, waiting to meet with Hillary Clinton's staff. She had long been cozy with the Clintons: her ex-husband, Tony Podesta, was also an established lobbyist in his own right, and her brother-in-law John Podesta had once been President Bill Clinton's chief of staff and now was running Hillary Clinton's 2016 campaign for the Oval Office. But these days actual politics was merely a footnote in her daily life—working for tech companies was far more lucrative.

With a shock of grey hair swirling through her salt-and-pepper bob, and wearing bright-red lipstick, she stood out in the lobby so much that John Podesta's eyes went right to her as he walked into the hotel. A number of Clinton staffers followed suit, acknowledging that they'd soon see her at the meeting that afternoon.

But for now, Heather, forty-six, was talking about the egg lobby. She was in the middle of fighting it—on behalf of the tech industry. In the past year, she had made over $7 million from lobbying, and hundreds of thousands of that had come from tech companies such as Snapchat, Zocdoc, Fitbit, and SpaceX. She was also representing a new food-tech company called Hampton Creek, whose product Just Mayo was enraging the egg lobby because it didn't contain eggs, yet claimed to be mayonnaise. In their view, nothing labeled "mayonnaise" should be egg free. To help argue its case, the egg lobby had hired "mommy bloggers" to spread rumors saying that Just Mayo wasn't safe, wasn't really mayo, and was a threat to the farmers of the United States.

Podesta was gearing up to prove that this technological mayo was, in fact, the real thing. If it tasted like mayo and looked like mayo, she argued, it was none of the egg people's business. And wouldn't there be a legislator who might rather have the backing of the tech industry than the egg industry? After all, which was more viable these days? Tech companies helped these lobbyists wield more power. The industry had deeper pockets, and its CEOs were often so young and innocent that they didn't even know how best to empty them.

Take Fitbit for example, a device that tracks steps and calories. How was the company of the same name to know that its product could soon be scrutinized by the FDA for carrying consumer data? Fitbit had to make sure its branding and marketing materials met FDA standards before it was too late, she explained as she showed off a sleek, black Fitbit on her wrist.

James Proud's company fell into that category. Lately, these lobbyists for incumbents such as the taxi and limousine commissions, the egg lobby, the meat lobby, and the auto dealers, to name

a few, were becoming more aware of these upstart start-ups earlier and earlier. It was a reason that Podesta suggested companies
hire her as soon as possible.

Uber's and then Airbnb's battles with the government in
order to be allowed into various markets were probably the most
public cases in which the tech industry came head-to-head with
a species opposite to them—government workers—in a really
do-or-die kind of way. Uber's triumph over the attempted regulations both inspired and terrified a host of other companies. But
at least it could be done—victory against one of the country's and
most cities' strongest unions—thanks to a young lobbyist by the
name of Bradley Tusk.

Tusk, forty-two, grew up in Brooklyn, New York, and then
went on to the University of Pennsylvania, where he became interested in politics early. In college, he got a job working for Philadelphia mayor Ed Rendell, whom he met after he got a ticket
to the Democratic convention through a friend in the carpenters'
union. He saw the mayor sitting alone. He sat next to him, started
chatting, and then showed up at his office to leave a note about
wanting an internship with him. He got it.

Tusk wasn't traditionally charismatic, but he had a familiar
way about him. He put you at ease. At a cafe across the street
from his New York office, he treated the waitstaff as if he'd known
them for years, even though he said it was one of the few times he
went there. These days, he represented companies such as Tesla

and FanDuel, DraftKings and Mytable, the latter a marketplace for locally cooked meals. But it was Uber that really made his name when Travis Kalanick offered him equity instead of cash in exchange for his help.

But that came much later. After Tusk left the Philadelphia mayor's office, he moved back home, where he worked for the New York City Department of Parks & Recreation. The commissioner then, Henry Stern, he recalled, "hired young, white Jewish men for twenty-two thousand dollars a year to basically run big chunks of the agency." After a stint in law school in Chicago, he went back to the Parks Department and then down to Washington, DC, where he worked as New York senator Charles Schumer's communications director for two years. "It was so crazy, because Chuck is the most media-hungry, aggressive member of Congress, and also 9/11 happened after my first year there," he remembered.

Then, when Michael Bloomberg was elected mayor of New York in 2001, Tusk left DC to work for him. Now that he could see how easily politicians could be manipulated through lobbying, he respected Bloomberg's unpopular decisions, made possible because he didn't need anyone's money to help get him reelected.

When Lehman filed for bankruptcy in 2008, he got another call from Michael Bloomberg, who asked him to help change the term limits for mayoralty in New York and organize his campaign for reelection. He came back to New York. Bloomberg won a third term. Tusk didn't stay on in the administration, however. Instead, he decided to start his own consulting firm, which would turn into five separate businesses: a venture business, a consulting business, an archive business in which he'd create digital archives for foundations such as the Rockefeller Foundation or high-net-worth individuals such as hedge fund manager Ken Griffin, as well as a casino business and a family foundation.

A few years later, Tusk got a call from the Illinois governor's office, asking him if he would be deputy governor of the state. So at age twenty-nine, he went to work for Governor Rod Blago-jevich, who was later convicted of corruption. "I think there's a benign reason I got hired and a less benign reason," he explained. The benign one was that Tusk was young enough that he figured Blagojevich assumed he would put up with working more than ninety hours a week. The less benign version was this: "I was a kid, and he could rob the place blind and I would never notice, which was also probably true." When Blagojevich was removed from office in 2009, much of the legislation Tusk had written had to be checked for validity. The governor was absent so often that the prosecutors doubted he had anything to do with any legisla-tion passed during his tenure.

That experience led Tusk to leave the public sector and go into business. He became familiar with the Chicago lottery sys-tem and decided he would figure out a way to make it more prof-itable and broadly appealing. So he took his idea to all of the big investment banks, saying that he wanted to build a business to privatize state lotteries. "Both rightly and wrongly, I picked the wrong bank, which was Lehman Brothers," he said. "They were totally true to their word, which is why I picked them, but they also took down the global economy."

His ability to branch out into that many areas was made possible through his Uber equity. One day in 2012, Tusk got a call from a small transportation start-up that the government was trying to shut down. It was Kalanick, who told him that he couldn't afford Tusk's fee but would pay him instead with stock. Tusk Strategies turned into Uber's first government relations department. It would run campaigns against city officials, such as New York City mayor Bill de Blasio, who wanted to support entrenched interests such as taxi medallions and limousines.

Now Tusk's other companies relied on him for the same thing. They would come to him and say, "I want to be like TK"—Travis Kalanick—to get past government hurdles in the same way. Until recently, Tusk thought, the tech industry had no idea how to deal with the government. As it started creating entire new industries and payment systems, there was no existing legislation for stand-alone car companies or stand-alone virtual currencies such as Bitcoin, for example. Tusk became a ready and willing go between.

One of Tusk's clients, Ripple, a distributed ledger company, was the underlying system that makes Bitcoin possible. In its case, he thought it would be beneficial for officials to regulate

Bitcoin, because he thought the intervention would help legitimize the business. A regulatory system would make customers more comfortable with the new currency and make Bitcoin seem like less of a currency outsider. "When you're trying to introduce a new currency, you need to know how to deal with the government," he said. "It's not true that every start-up just wants to avoid regulation at all costs; some want to be left alone, some want an even playing field—it's totally dependent on each start-up." With regulations, both parties could benefit, he thought. "What if you could pay your taxes in Bitcoin, or parking meters in Bitcoin?" Tusk asked. "What if the government could use Bitcoin to pay for things too?"

Tusk would run the strategies for each company like he would a political campaign. He worked with both the government and the industry side by side after all. As he was working with his eight tech companies, he was also putting together Bloomberg's unlikely and later abandoned presidential bid as an independent in early 2016.

Tusk wanted politicians to start seeing tech companies as donors and their customers as voters. The five million people who played FanDuel, an online fantasy sports site, for example, voted, and might not like New York attorney general Eric Schneiderman capping their usage. They might not look too kindly on him if he were to run for a new position someday. Public schools might not have liked AltSchool, a technology-driven "microschool," but parents who weren't pleased with their children's education options also voted.

Tusk enjoyed the fight. "We just basically kicked the shit out of the mayor and the taxi industry until they backed down," he remembered of his fight on behalf of Uber during the summer of 2015. He would do the same for Tesla against the auto dealers who tried to get the electric car company regulated because Teslas were sold directly to consumers, bypassing dealers. It was a matter of assessing a company's business goal and coming up with a way to achieve that while fighting off any policies that might be in the way. Tusk took a multipronged approach. Every morning, each client was emailed a detailed strategy listing all the tactics that would be used that day.

"Our view is unless we're bringing the intensity of a political campaign, nothing gets done," he said. "Uber, in many ways, was the beginning of it because even though there was the Google and Microsoft suit in the 1990s, those companies had these big federal issues; it was one issue with one federal agency about privacy or market domination. But Uber was a totally new way of doing something," he explained. "They were pissing off an entrenched interest with every city that's politically active." Uber, he thought, was the first instance of the new norm.

For Tusk and his companies, it was only a matter of time before each new company would need to deal with the government. The question, he said, was, "When do you beg for forgiveness, and when do you ask for permission?" For those with passionate customers, it was easier to wait until a company had to beg forgiveness from the government because by then, it had built up a ready group of defenders. Once the newcomer did decide to fight, it took grassroots emails, legislature targeting, and placing stories in papers such as the *San Francisco Chronicle, New York Times*, and *Los Angeles Times*.

For fights like Uber to stay in Las Vegas, for example, the customers often had to pitch in with petitions to fight one of the most powerful taxi unions in the country. Luckily for Uber, tourists familiar with using the service in their home cities were eager to argue that they should stay there because Uber made their vacations easier.

In some markets, particularly Las Vegas, "The structure is very friendly to incumbent interests," said Tusk. The medallion owners and unions were known for their campaign contributions and tried to use that to reinforce the status quo. "We might be fighting a particular legislator who is in the pocket of the auto dealers," he explained. He said it happened all the time.

Tech companies, however, were largely unfamiliar with the political favor game. They were far away from Washington, DC, first of all, and second of all, the founders weren't naturally political. Engineering geeks barely knew how to make friends or navigate a cocktail party, let alone be politically manipulative. There was also an ingrained idea that the tech industry could solve everything and that the government wasn't necessary. Of course, there were exceptions, and those were some of the successes. Tusk was trying to change those habits. He wanted tech companies to become familiar with how to handle politicians—that give-and-take would benefit both parties, he thought. He admitted that it would probably be a ten-to-twenty-year process to get tech companies used to the idea.

For now, Tusk was thinking of the short term. He wanted to make sure that each of his companies could still operate, and then he would worry about the laws that would keep them in business in the long term. He hoped to someday influence the laws around self-driving cars, as well as shape public opinion about them. He wanted to make sure that Uber didn't have to face any new game-changing regulations. Next, he was getting on a call with AirMap, a coordinating body for drones. Tusk wasn't even sure he understood the revenue model, or if drones even had one yet, but he wanted to get in at the beginning.

Drones, recreational and commercial, were an entirely new world. Would FedEx fight them? Would they be safe for consumers? Would they be used for war? Who owned the airspace in which to fly them? "No one's ever thought about it before," he said. "There may not be an evil egg industry or taxi cartel, but there will be something."

Otherwise, Tusk said, he tried to avoid young seed-stage companies. He would instead wait until the company was big enough to need him to mount a fight. A company needed time to grow and then later mobilize an enthusiastic customer base so that he could get the job done. With Uber, at least, the customers' experiences with the cars was often so much better than with the local taxi industry—the incumbent—that as early as 2012, they were able to sign up a hundred thousand customers to go to city hall in New York to argue for the government to leave Uber alone. FanDuel had the same public support. "I think it's pretty rare to build a product that people are that passionate about," he said.

Generally speaking, Tusk found entrepreneurs in the San Francisco Bay Area to be in denial about their weaknesses in the face of government regulation. He considered many of the companies that approached him too arrogant about their potential to stay off the radar of the law. So many founders, he said, would scoff, "I went to Stanford, then I went to Y Combinator, so when the stupid regulators see my business plan, *of course* they'll do what I want because I'm so special!" He found that attitude prevalent through the tech industry.

The other problem was that many start-ups didn't even realize who their future enemies would be. For example, the meat industry put up a huge fight to quash food companies that came up with substitute hamburger—products that would never even appeal to meat eaters.

Tusk, though biased, was starting to find that companies

whose customers were aware of their cooperation with the government tended to have better public perceptions. He didn't approve of Apple's refusal to comply with the FBI to hack into the San Bernardino shooter's iPhone. "What I worry about is Apple looks in some ways so cavalier that your average taxi regulator thinks, 'These effing start-ups, they're arrogant,' and it hurts all my companies." He thought that Apple was hurting start-ups in more regulated situations.

These days, he contended, tech companies no longer existed in a single industry anyway; *all* new companies were tech companies. And most companies in general were regulated. "A tech company is no different than Amazon; something delivered to your door," he said. "There are a lot of opportunities for us these days."

Young James Proud's promotional materials reflected Sense's ability to track and manage sleep rather than to help people sleep or counter insomnia. Instead, he positioned it as a wellness device, not a product that could provide some kind of prescriptive fix. All branding materials now are more general, hinting at possible new uses for the Sense tracker, such as using it to enhance athletic performance—or as home décor.

For the most part, the Thiel fellows had yet to brush up against the government in any real way. Laura Deming's life-extending drug research was still in the laboratory, so dealing with the FDA was years away. Plus, she didn't have to tackle regulation directly. She could decide which biotech companies to invest in based on the likelihood of their eventual approval.

At least Silicon Valley was generating enough new technologies and new science in entirely new fields without any prior incumbents. In many cases, there was no existing industry to disrupt. While technology replaced existing jobs, it also created brand-new fields. Artificial intelligence, for instance, would be a whole new headache for government regulators as well as entrepreneurs—and society. Suddenly, thanks to Silicon Valley, new areas of thought, ethics, and laws would have to be crafted. These go-betweens such as Bradley Tusk were now at the center.

11

Is This Really Right?

While the baby companies of Thiel fellows such as James Proud and Paul Gu had their growing pains—with Proud still trying to get the tracker made at scale, and Gu rejiggering his business model over and over again—they were comfortably navigating Silicon Valley, if not as stars, then at least as survivors. John Burnham wasn't finding the same fate.

By fall 2014, the twenty-one-year-old wasn't sure he liked what he saw there. As he struggled to launch Urbit, a personal server platform, he was often frustrated with how little the valley's hierarchy valued the actual people who built the products or used them. Whether it was due in part to the convoluted nature of his company, which neither he nor his cofounder, Curtis Yarvin, could seem to explain in English, Burnham was feeling more and more detached. He felt like his reason for being out there was to build a company that would get a mythical high valuation, which he didn't think would come from anything like his own merit or character. And what did Silicon Valley think character was, anyway? Were they even aware of it? If Gu's company was giving it the value of a statistic on an Excel spreadsheet, what did that mean?

Burnham felt like the valley's attitude toward what it meant to be human wasn't that different from what it meant to function as a machine. Philosophically, this idea didn't sit well with him. It didn't fit into his basic sense of right and wrong. No matter that it was also a convenient reason for why none of his companies was really working for him. Maybe he was just too moral, too principled, and too ethically correct. And now he wasn't getting along with his cofounder.

The qualities that had made him interested in Yarvin, otherwise known as his blogosphere hero Mencius Moldbug, he found odious in person. The man was stubborn and intractable. He didn't really turn his ideas into reality, and they certainly didn't translate into financial success.

Yarvin-Moldbug was to have given a presentation at the annual Strange Loop programming conference in 2015, but was booted months before the conference because of his libertarian, non–politically correct viewpoints, such as his argument to do away with democracy in favor of monarchy or dictatorship. Yarvin was spending more time riding that wave of fame than working on Urbit. Oddly for Silicon Valley, each owned 50 percent of the stock. It meant that should a disagreement arise, they were stuck. They couldn't move forward, since neither had more power than the other.

Reading Yarvin's contrarian posts and following his philosophy online was one thing; listening to it all day was another. Plus, Burnham seemed to think because of his young age and his Thiel Fellowship, along with his previous experience attempting three other start-ups—a badge of honor in Silicon Valley—the engineering expertise would be easier to pick up. Urbit was centered on computer science.

But Burnham much preferred reading books and writing. Plus, Urbit was having trouble raising money—though it recently raised $200,000, well after Burnham had left. The company hadn't gone anywhere since its initial burst of blogosphere attention while Burnham was still at Dartmouth. John missed the East Coast. He missed his parents—and having means. He wasn't wild about the rut he was falling into (along with camping out at the office), and he was feeling increased pressure to have something to show for his long stay out west.

So Burnham gave up and decided to head back to Dartmouth. It was an odd return. He felt funny having to explain himself again to the other students. "It was a little bit embarrassing," he remembered. It was like he'd come back a failure, after leaving campus the first time after two weeks to pursue his dream. Plus, at twenty-two, he was older than everyone else.

In New England, especially at Dartmouth, sports and fraternities were king, not hackathons and start-up clubs. He'd become so used to the forward, game-to-meet-anyone attitude of Silicon Valley that being back on a college campus where there were already cliques and crews with their own habits and social calendars left him unsure of what to do with himself. John stuck it out at Dartmouth for a term and a half but didn't feel comfortable there. He didn't find the classes challenging enough, either. So at the end of spring term, he went on leave to attend a tiny Catholic liberal arts college in New Hampshire called Thomas More College. It was the only place where he felt like he fit in. There, bright and hardworking kids who didn't really have a place in normal university life and were interested in the humanities came to burrow away on campus and study philosophy.

Classes were much harder there than at Dartmouth too. On break from Thomas More, he recalled a course at Dartmouth on William Shakespeare's play *Hamlet*. He said the professor adored him because he had done the reading. "That was the whole course," he said. "The only requirement was to read *Hamlet* and write three papers, and show up to class once in a while." Burnham didn't see the point.

At Thomas More, he read *The Iliad* and *The Odyssey*, Plato's *The Republic*, and Aristophanes's *The Clouds*. He took Greek literature. He saw it as a needed retreat from the madness he'd just experienced out west. It was the anti–Silicon Valley.

What was really different, he thought, was the spiritual focus of the school. Burnham had never been religious, but here he found solace in religion. "Everyone is very much on the same page in terms of values and the goal of education," he said. "I think that's an essential basis, that you have to have shared values and shared ways of looking at the world." Thomas More was so small that it had only two dorms: a male dorm and a female dorm. Although they weren't nearly as nice as the dorms at Dartmouth, Burnham liked them better. "I think that roughing it a little bit is really excellent for building character and community," he said. "Although I miss the elevator at Dartmouth."

It was the opposite of the Thiel Fellowship in more ways than one. First of all, everyone did the same thing all together. They all went to Rome, all took the same classes and tutorials, and all did the same reading—often about the lives of the saints. Those ancient thinkers, he said, answered more questions for him than the people in Silicon Valley did. There, he said, he often wondered what was the purpose of the start-ups that employed him. Were the tech companies actually making the world a better place? he wondered. "Is this going to be a net gain for the human experience or a net harm?" he asked himself. John realized later that the only way those questions were answerable was if you had some kind of basis for assessing what "the good life" really was, or "what the purpose of man's existence is."

Burnham didn't think Silicon Valley particularly cared about those questions. He thought its perspectives were varied, from utilitarian to commercial, but the only criterion was whether a company was profitable. "It's not a complete picture of people and what people are," he said. "So I guess for me, what formed my decision to go along a different path, is that I had a lot of questions, and I wanted to answer them, and I wanted to devote some time and serious study to figuring out why certain things occur; why do they happen, and what can we do about it?"

In Silicon Valley, said Burnham, "It's just a really interesting phenomenon that if you're running the company that does nothing, you can feel like king of the world." People felt they were accomplishing things anyway. "If it's smoke, then there are people who go from smoke to smoke to smoke, and they have a successful track record."

He saw a lot of companies selling things they didn't really have—just marketing products for hype. "In a way, that's a kind of manipulative thing," he said. "It's one thing if you've really got something and want to bring it to the world, but I think it's another thing if you don't have anything, and you're trying to raise hype and thereby sort of growing nothing really big."

Looking back, though, John said he wouldn't change his

course. "I don't really know if I can second-guess the decisions I made. I was a really different person when I was eighteen, so if I had to make those decisions over again, I might, but I wouldn't have known if I hadn't made them." At Thomas More, Burnham was starting over as a freshman. He'd be about twenty-five when he graduated. "It's a very strange thing," he said, especially since the whole point of the Thiel Fellowship was to start out in the real world earlier than usual, not later.

Silicon Valley, he said, had given him a new perspective on the world. A different breed of person fueled technological innovation, he discovered. It was a single-mindedness that he wasn't so sure he had. Some of their acute focus didn't point in the same direction he wanted to go. "How the world of technology sees itself and the rest of the world helps you understand a lot of what's changing," he reflected. He thought that technological tools that replaced tasks that people used to do by hand, such as writing letters or sending Christmas cards, or putting photographs in a physical album, were a little bit sad.

All that had been digitized was now stored in the mysterious ether. "Having been in that world, I know how the sausage is made, and parts of it are not really all that pretty," he said. It bothered him that the data people gave to these new tools and toys were no longer theirs. "Their control over it is vastly smaller than what they're used to, but if you have photo albums, no one can look unless they get a warrant from a judge," said Burnham. "If you've got photos on Facebook, or make some post, that's gone into some enormously complex system that no one really understands." It reflected a world, he thought, that was going from intelligible to complex and unintelligible. He quoted the science fiction writer Arthur C. Clarke, author of *2001: A Space Odyssey*: "Any sufficiently advanced technology is indistinguishable from magic."

Sometimes the magic went to people's heads. "I think there's a real attitude in the tech industry that they know better than the rest of the world, or the government, or, let's say, other industries," he said. Those in the start-up world thought everyone else didn't do anything as efficiently as they did. Sometimes they were right. But Burnham often found that this attitude was backed only in theory rather than reality. Look at his own experience. His dreams of asteroid mining attracted a lot of attention and sounded good, but he could never attract any investors or think of a practical way to actually travel to the asteroids and then mine them for minerals. He saw a lot of companies having the same problem, where they promised some sort of magic but had a difficult time delivering, such as Theranos with its revolutionary blood test device that wasn't.

12

We Will Be God

In Silicon Valley, much of this "magic" centered on artificial intelligence. AI was spoken of like a futuristic Merlin: a wizard who would someday descend upon the human race and turn everyone into high-functioning robots. That was one school of thought, at least. There were those who believed humans would "evolve" into machine-like creatures—cyborgs—enhanced by technology, with software that would program certain aspects of biological and cognitive functions. Then there were those who shared the humanistic view, in which humans used technology to make themselves better humans, even *more* human. They sounded similar, but they were two different mentalities, and there were two different groups of people who believed in each.

In some respects, belief in artificial intelligence's capabilities was divided into evolutionary AI and humanistic AI. Evolutionary artificial intelligence aficionados believed that machines would take over humans; that men and women were innately weak and full of imperfections, and that eventually a smarter, more intelligent machine would replace our meek human capabilities and guilt-ridden consciences (for such crimes as environmental degradation, violence, sexism) and make our species more effective and enlightened.

Humanists who studied AI weren't often in San Francisco, but those who were believed in its ability to empower humans. In their view, humans could use their superior brainpower to master and harness the machines, never giving up their own qualia, or command of the humanities, emotions, and uniquely human attributes. They would use technology only to function at a higher level; to become more efficient, such as by making superior software and completing more tasks. But unlike the evolutionary camp's point of view, computers wouldn't replace or enhance or affect human feelings in any way.

The AI humanists left the intention with people. They left faith and higher purpose to God, more often than not. They had a capitalist view of artificial intelligence that sought to make what was already good—human intelligence—better, with additional machine learning; whereas evolutionary AI proponents thought feelings and emotions all boiled down to neurons firing as electric currents did in a computer anyway.

By reducing humans to machines, and then allowing machines to take them over, it was a way to make everyone equal again: a socialist worldview in which we were all just bunches of cells and neurons, no one was better than the next person, and one person had merely another, possibly luckier, reconfiguration of cells than another. To them, it was madness to think there were innate differences between people, even in terms of intelligence, since the first intelligence machine would have the power to be more intelligent than the most intelligent human.

The two kingpins of each of these movements lived on opposite coasts. Ray Kurzweil, the futurist and author of *The Singularity Is Near: When Humans Transcend Biology*, represented the West Coast evolutionary AI figures (though they would never call themselves that), while David Gelernter, based at Yale University, was one of the few, albeit influential, humanist artificial intelligence experts. Humanists were more attuned to the danger that artificial intelligence posed, not in terms of "evil AI" or computers gone rogue in satanic opposition to their positive AI God, but in terms of what the rise of machines would mean for the fall of humanity. Some truly believed AI was dangerous, threatening to eradicate the values that make us human. They considered life ingredients such as art, family, and culture as individual urges with intentions that made life worth living. They didn't think computers could replicate that idea of human progress, human reason, or our noble cause.

In Silicon Valley, the phrase "changing of the world" had become a cliché. But in recent years, it had turned into changing of the species, though no one could say that line enough to turn it into a cliché. For what they were doing was turning the idea of changing what it meant to be human into a measurement.

That wasn't so in New York. There, those in high places clung to what made humans human for centuries. Hedge fund managers who made it turned Fifth Avenue townhouses into ancient palazzos, they got grand pianos like they used to see in their fantastical visions of robber barons' high-flying lives, such as the late Salomon Brothers head John Gutfreund, who once had a twenty-two-foot-tall Norwegian Christmas tree hoisted into his apartment through a balcony window. They went on long weekends to grouse hunts in England, even if they grew up spending Saturdays at the Short Hills Mall in suburban New Jersey. It was a retrowealth, a harkening back to what it was to be human *last* century.

Across the country, this century was passé, let alone last. Who cared about the birds? How backward to fly across an ocean to go shoot them in funny-looking, uncomfortable outfits. In the Bay Area, the focus was on human evolution, and the next step seemed to be through this increasingly realistic literal marriage of man and machine. The greater ambition was a different kind of goal: not to buy the most expensive houses, cars, and boats, or be invited to the most exclusive parties, but to change the species into its highest iteration.

Of course, they still wanted the party invites too. But by 2016, they were finally media darlings, with Sean Parker and Elon Musk and Larry Page not only invited but *entreated* to come to high-end events such as the *Vanity Fair* Oscar party and the Costume Institute Ball hosted by *Vogue* editor Anna Wintour at New York's Metropolitan Museum of Art. (Oh, and could you make a donation too?) So that was all set. They were now free to focus on higher matters.

Onward! Time to disrupt, transgress, and reengineer— themselves and humanity as a whole. While some of the Silicon Valley gods considered species improvement an underlying goal, they couldn't say it out loud. Instead, their minions would have to work on it through secret projects or through safe organizations where it was okay to talk about. At Singularity University, the singularity wasn't just near, it was imminent. Ray Kurzweil was their king. He had a cult following.

Kurzweil believed that people would eventually stay young, ideally around age thirty, for hundreds of years. He conceded that living that way could get boring, so he explained away that phenomenon by saying that along with inevitable radical life extension would come radical life expansion, with new experiences, knowledge, music, and literature. He thought artificial intelligence would enable us to take our lives into our own hands with endless choices that would go on forever. If you were killed in a car accident, you had already backed up your mind and body, so could be re-created. He wasn't joking! This way, we had more options at all times, he thought. Instead of death giving life meaning, he believed that culture, creating, music, and science gave it meaning. "Death interrupts science," he said.

To prepare for this upcoming event, he treated his body as a complex machine, downing 250 pills a day, sitting in a lab getting hormone drips one day a week, and drinking gallons of green tea daily. In 2013 the sixty-five-year-old inventor moved closer to the hotbed of where all the technological activity was happening. He left his home outside of Boston, where he lived in a Newton mansion lined with Marc Chagall paintings and holograms of Cheshire cats, to go to Silicon Valley to work at Google. What Kurzweil did there wasn't secret, but how he planned on building humanity a new neocortex was. He hoped to upload human brains and expand them through technology, eventually allowing humans and computers to merge as one—in year 2045. That was when human intelligence would be enhanced a billionfold thanks to high-tech brain extensions.

For now, in 2015, he was working as a director of engineering, primarily getting machines to understand what scientists called "natural" language. Computers still weren't as good as humans at figuring out the context of questions and speech. They could scan the words in an article and 56 percent of the time figure out that Barack Obama was the president of the United States, while a human would read the same article and reach that conclusion with near certainty. Kurzweil was developing software that he hoped would enable computers to understand language conceptually rather than just by key words—with the near-term goal of creating a better, more conversational search function for Google.

But the inventor had made the unlikely possible before. He had invented the first print-to-speech reading machine for the blind, just to start. But it was his bestselling books *The Age of Spiritual Machines: When Computers Exceed Human Intelligence* (2000) and *The Singularity Is Near* (2005) that really made his name. In *How to Create a Mind: The Secret of Human Thought Revealed*, published in 2012, he described how to build a synthetic extension of the brain that would connect it to the cloud. He thought that nanobots would travel one day to our brains through our capillaries and that blood-cell-sized computers would connect to the cloud the same way that iPhones do.

Before the publication of *How to Create a Mind*, Kurzweil met with Google's then CEO Larry Page to give him a copy and pitch him on investing in a company he wanted to create based on the ideas in his book. Page was interested but instead persuaded Kurzweil to start it at Google, having the use of the company's resources while maintaining his independence. (Since then, Google has continued building a veritable artificial intelligence laboratory, hiring artificial intelligence researcher Geoffrey Hinton and in 2014 acquiring the British company DeepMind Technologies—renaming it Google DeepMind—which combines techniques from machine learning and neuroscience to build algorithms. But Google, of course, went apoplectic when Kurzweil spoke these thoughts out loud; the company wanted to separate his ideas from Google's mission and goals. God forbid it reflect on its own aspirations, which certainly were not publicly reengineering humans, its valuable customers.)

Some of Kurzweil's ideas hit the mainstream. Spike Jonze, the director of *Her*, the 2013 film about a man who forms a relationship with an intelligent (and female-sounding) operating system, has said that Kurzweil's writings inspired him to write, direct, and produce the movie. Still, Kurzweil found some fault in the film's development of the futuristic operating system, voiced by Scarlett Johansson. With her high level of emotional understanding, he said, she also should have had a virtual body.

These days, Kurzweil's actual body looks its age, even with his intravenous nutrient intake and "real age" of forty. He still wants to reprogram our biology as well, which he said began with the Human Genome Project and included regenerating tissue through stem cell therapies and the 3-D printing of new organs.

Kurzweil was well aware of the darker side of a more technological future. "Technology has always been a double-edged sword," he said. Fire helped humans improve their lives, but it also burnt down villages. And while he thought that technology could reprogram our biology away from disease, it could also fall into the hands of terrorists who might reprogram colds into deadly viruses. ("We're not defenseless against that," he added, having spent time helping the US Army come up with a program to combat biological threats.) However, he was reassured by the ubiquity of networked technology. With smartphones in the hands of billions of people, crowds could organize to deal with many problems, he thought.

In any case, Kurzweil planned to be around to see whatever the future held. "The goal is to live indefinitely," he insisted. As a backup plan, he would preserve his body cryogenically. But, he said, "The goal is not to need to."

Across the country at Yale, another computer scientist who knew his fair share about artificial intelligence, David Gelernter, considered Kurzweil the Antichrist, seeing mostly the darker side of his contemporary's vision. Gelernter found Kurzweil's predictions not only depressing and nihilistic but also dangerous.

After all, Gelernter was not a typical computer scientist. Most days, he stood at an easel near a wide window in his Woodbridge, Connecticut, home and painted. His two pet parrots flew around a house filled with stacks of books and papers. The birds screeched sporadically, and every now and then one popped up from behind the couch to say "Peekaboo." There were no gadgets in sight, aside from a desktop computer barely visible in an adjacent office.

"I hate computers, and I refuse to play with them," he said, as he geared up to write one of his many attacks on Kurzweil, this next one called "The Closing of the Scientific Mind." "Any success I've had in computing is because I fit so badly in the field," he explained with a laugh. He thought that using computers should be more logical. "I want software to work in thirty seconds," he said.

Gelernter had just launched a new company called Lifestreams. It was an attempt to make computers more human rather than the other way around. Lifestreams would make desktops more intuitive and narrative. The information would be chronological, not disseminated throughout a blue screen in the form of icons and confusing dropdown menus.

Years ago, a first try at commercializing his ideas ended in failure, but Gelernter was used to setbacks. In 1993 he was the target of a mail bomb from Theodore "Ted" Kaczynski, known as the Unabomber, who between 1978 and 1995 conducted a campaign of domestic terrorism against people involved in developing technology. The explosion disfigured Gelernter's right hand and blinded his right eye. He wrote the book *Drawing Life: Surviving the Unabomber* in 1997 about living through the trauma. Nearly ten years later, Gelernter was still physically uncomfortable. He moved around his living room slowly but didn't complain about his ailments.

He was troubled that people would describe the Unabomber as "sick" or a disturbed "genius" yet hesitated to call him "evil." It prompted Gelernter to ask, "What does it mean when a culture no longer believes in evil?" and "What happens to a society that has lost its ability to react morally in a crisis?"

In *Drawing Life*, Gelernter turned his own pain, disfigurement, and subsequent recovery into a metaphor for the state of the country. He criticized the United States for losing the resources that helped him to mend—religion, family, art—and argued that American culture focused on sensationalizing crime rather than on teaching courage and character.

Artificial intelligence, he thought, was incapable of knowing about character, or bravery, or anything that made us qualitatively human. Gelernter's personal slogan for his company was "By humans for humans." Humanity, he thought, would never be replaced by machines. Our subjective, conscious experiences could never be programmed, he said. With what we knew so far about computers, he said, there was no way they could ever be conscious. They didn't get built—or turn on, even—without human intent.

If humans had built computers to be helpers of humanity, he thought, he never would have had to restart his old company to make them more intuitive. In the 1990s, Mirror Worlds Technologies never got off the ground commercially and ran out of money in 2004. Ironically, Gelernter started seeing his early ideas pop up in Apple products. He believed that three of Apple's features—Cover Flow, Time Machine, and Spotlight, for flipping through CD covers, backing up files, and performing searches, respectively—looked like the software he had invented. Although Gelernter never sued Apple himself, a lawyer discovered an email that had been sent by the late Apple founder and CEO Steve Jobs to a handful of his lieutenants about Mirror Worlds, saying, "It may be something for our future, and we may want to secure a license ASAP." (Apple never did get a license.)

That sentence became the basis of a lawsuit filed by Mirror World's patent holders. (Gelernter and his coinventor, Eric Freeman, had sold their patent as a condition of the company's funding in the 1990s, though Gelernter retains a 2 percent stake, minus costs, in any award from the lawsuit. Gelernter never saw the email from Jobs until the trial itself.) In 2010 a jury voted in favor of Mirror Worlds and gave its patent holders $625 million in damages, one of the top five patent awards in US history. Six months later, however, a judge overruled the verdict. An appeal was unsuccessful, and in June 2013 the US Supreme Court declined to hear the case. Finally, in July 2016, Apple paid a $25 million settlement for the Cover Flow and Time Machine patents.

Still, Gelernter admitted that his ideas might not have been viable a decade ago anyway. Apple could have just made use of them at the right time. "The technology was not ready, the graphics weren't ready, and people's state of mind was not ready." Now he thinks the world may be able to see his vision. "It was F. Scott Fitzgerald who said there are no second acts in American lives," he said. "But this is a second act."

Whether or not he could stop Ray Kurzweil and his ilk was another matter. But by trying to change the direction of the way artificial intelligence would be used, Gelernter hoped to sway people away from the idea that humans would evolve into robots, and help them reclaim individual will and identity. Gelernter's anti-Kurzweil world view is put forth less in his software than in his book *The Tides of Mind* (2016).

John Burnham fell on the more humanist side of the spectrum. "The concern with AI is that AI is a machine," he said. "People created it with a utility function set of values, which sounds all well and good, but that assumes that intelligence is enslaved to a utility function set of values, and assumes those two ideas are compatible—that you can have intelligent being without free will. But the only example of an intelligent being—us—is one that has free will."

By 2016, Burnham had swung so far in the direction of the qualia, that religion was guiding his choices now more than ever. The following year, he would become confirmed as Catholic. (After a year at Thomas More he returned to Dartmouth, in fall 2016, to study math.) Silicon Valley, he said, had given him an entirely new perspective on humanity, one that made him value what it actually meant to be conscious—as a human in particular. He was now fixated on all that was nonprogrammable about us.

At Thomas More College, he wrote an essay on human

beings' unique perspective on time. In some ways it was the flip-side of Kurzweil's ideas, but not entirely dissimilar:

"Man cannot by nature be purely body, since he is not fully explicable through the corporeal. Man apprehends, at least in some small way, part of Divine revelation. To an angel, a being living in Eternity, prophetic revelation is irrelevant, since they perceive the whole of Time at once. To an animal, not possessing the means to imagine forms outside of time, prophetic revelation is impossible. Man is uniquely defined as being, according to Aquinas, 'composed of soul and body,' and this union is exemplified most clearly in those phenomena that comprise the intersection of the Eternal and the Temporal. Man is the only creature that can both look out of Time at Eternity and, through revelation, look into Time from Eternity."

From an inverse vantage point, Kurzweil echoed Burnham's thoughts. "Soon we'll live forever, take over the universe, control the universe," he said. Singularity, he said, would make us closer to the supernatural. Already he could teleport, after all—at least as a hologram. "The universe is not very intelligent, so eventually we'll take over the solar system, and in essence we'll be Godlike." He popped another one of his supplement pills, and got in his Lexus hybrid proto-self-driving car. Once we break the speed of light, "We'll be closer to God than ever before," he said as he careened around a corner onto the highway. "We will be God."

Conclusion

Of the first class of 2011 fellows, including Laura Deming, John Burnham, Paul Gu, and James Proud, only about one in ten ended up going back to college, according to Danielle Strachman, the program's original director. But when that did happen, she said, the fellows did it in a determined way. Eden Full created the SunSaluter solar panel system, but she had always planned to return to Princeton University. When Full got back, however, she was so tired of the required courses, such as rhetoric and cultural studies—an idea she certainly had experienced firsthand during her travels to Africa—that she ended up dropping out again.

Most of the fellows who went back to school, Strachman said, used the academic experience for a reason: to apply it to something else they were working on as entrepreneurs. "What we saw was really deliberate," she emphasized.

Some, however, went back for the structure and social life. Noor Siddiqui, Burnham's ex-girlfriend who tried to start a charity company to combat poverty, felt she was missing out on college and the friendships it could provide. While frat parties were never her thing, she was afraid of being out on the loose, away from home, without a successful company, at least so far.

Noor's first idea had been the ambitious goal of trying to end poverty—the idea she applied with, in which she'd match poor people in third world countries to Western employers. But then, a year into her fellowship, she came up with a new company called Remedy, inspired by her sister's complaints that as a med school student, she thought more should be done medically in an ambulance on the way to the hospital versus at the hospital.

Her next idea entailed emergency responders using Google Glass, eyeglasses that had browsing and wireless capabilities, or their cell phones to allow doctors in hospitals to see what's happening in the ambulance and provide live support to the paramedics. The mobile display would send videos, images, and GPS, so that the physicians could respond remotely as to what form of treatment could be initiated en route.

In April 2014 Siddiqui started testing the system at Harvard and the University of Pennsylvania. The technology, to be called Beam, would assign numbers to patients in ambulances and then create an interface for surgeon supervisors. With one tap of a mobile phone, she said, an expert could see what was happening remotely. It would be the first product Remedy would put out. Eventually it would make wearable health care technology, but first the company was working with Google Glass. That way, she hoped to go beyond emergency situations to allow doctors to be able to see more patients more often in places without access to decent medical care. But still, Beam was slow to take off, and Noor wasn't raising the amount of capital she needed. The nineteen-year-old decided to go back to school and enroll at Stanford University while she attempted to keep her company going on the side.

She and Burnham were still in touch every now and then, and she called him before she made her decision to go to college. Her choice was somewhat influenced by his—to go to Dartmouth— even though that wasn't where he ended up.

After a low period out west, John Marbach, who had originally tried to build an online education platform, had also gone back to college, at Wake Forest in North Carolina. He wished he'd stayed in school all along. But he was among the few. The other fellows were still trying to make it in the tech industry, with varying degrees of success.

The biggest success story, actually, was based in India: Ritesh Agarwal, a young 2013 Thiel fellow whose line of budget hotel rooms, Oyo Rooms, was valued in 2016 at around $400 million. Another was Dylan Field, a 2012 Thiel fellow and former Brown University student who had raised nearly $18 million to start Figma, a company that was supposed to compete with Adobe Acrobat.

In the end, the Thiel fellowship has become reflective of the inherent cycles of Silicon Valley, or any area immersed in the uncertainties of entrepreneurship. Like the many PC makers before them or the search engines that came before Google, few succeeded but most did not. The program was a microcosm of the history of the area. The 2011 class hadn't fared as well financially as Agarwal and Field, save for Proud and Gu. Dale Stephens had capitulated to the idea that kids still wanted to go to college. He changed his UnCollege program into a gap-year program rather than a replacement of university. His site and seminars offered advice on how to tell your parents why you wanted to take a gap year rather than go straight to college, with points such as "Have a plan." It encouraged students to "intellectually misbehave."

Stephens asked, "Why not spend that time understanding who you are and what you want to do with life?" before entering college. His program cost $16,000, including room and board. Coaches taught students what they wanted to learn based on their own preferences. "Learning in its pure form is not for everyone," he conceded. "Some people want some guidance."

Some colleges offered credit for his program, but most admissions officers rolled their eyes. While Stephens had become one of the best-known Thiel fellows, he'd had a hard time raising money. He thought that venture capitalists preferred funding companies with big ideas and high valuations rather than those with cash flow, which he purported to have, claiming, "We were making money and delivering a product or service. We don't just have an algorithm." It was easier for him to raise money back east, actually, where investors wanted to see a bottom line.

Danielle Strachman was all too aware of this phenomenon. Having worked with frustrated fellows for five years, she was eager to move on to try her own hand at it. In early 2015 she left the fellowship to start her own fund for young entrepreneurs. It was called the 1517 Fund, in reference to the Protestant Reformation, alluding to Martin Luther's claim that the Church shouldn't be charging people to have a relationship with God. She thought that was the ethos of the fellowship too. People could pray to their own gods, or none. Maybe they could even *be* them. Looking back on the Thiel Fellowship, Strachman thought that it had changed the conversation about higher education and its importance.

"When it first started, we didn't know how big the ripple effect would be," she said. "People took a step back to truly think about the debt." Strachman thought the higher-education bubble had long been the elephant in the room, but "Peter pointed a very large finger at it."

Strachman also talked in Girardian terms. (René Girard, a French philosopher, believed in mimetic theory, the idea that people want what others *desire*, not what they have.) She called the fellowship a "mimetic mind blow." When it started, people weren't talking about dropping out of school. Anyone who did, she thought, would be considered a failure. Now, said Strachman, the higher-education bubble was a normal topic to discuss, and the program helped make that conversation possible.

"I think it's different but it's no longer weird. Those twenty people really made a huge difference in the lives of so many young people, particularly US based, since the cost of school here is so prohibitive." They showed, she believed, that college wasn't the only path and that people could learn by doing. "It's really about the optionality."

She considered the first class of fellows (2011) the bravest. They helped form the basis of the program and figured out what the structure could be so that it would define self-directed learning. The whole idea was a blank slate. Strachman said she didn't want the program to be coercive but more like a community that made decisions together. "It's not like a function where something goes into it and something comes out of it," she explained.

At the same time that the fellows were building companies, they were developing as people. "It wasn't like a thirty-year-old doing this who's been independent for a while," she pointed out. "We had people who were sixteen through nineteen starting, so during that first year, we did quarterly reviews of them. We knew we wanted to check in regularly." Later, they integrated the fellows into the process of choosing new fellows. They came up with organized events such as skydiving and motorcycle safety course outings. The fellows would do the planning, and the Thiel Foundation would pay the social costs.

After a while, the number of applicants far exceeded the available spots, so Strachman started the Thiel Summit series, where promising entrepreneurs who were viable for the fellowship could come meet one another. One Indian entrepreneur decided to sell his guitar and iPad to afford the flight to San Francisco. They added more interactive events such as lunches and evening meetings.

Strachman thought this interaction had become increasingly important. She also noticed that the conversation about human interaction, compatibility, and emotion had increased over the course of the five years of the fellowship—and had become a greater concern throughout Silicon Valley in general. When they were forming companies, people soon realized that their selection of coworkers was even more important than the technology they were developing.

Danielle thought that the success of Elon Musk's space company, SpaceX, had a huge impact on young people's aspirations.

"People look up to SpaceX and what is happening and see what you can do. Elon can go from PayPal to hard technology—to space—so it's amazing having ringleaders doing big and grand things."

Patri Friedman had also left the foundation. After his split from his wife, he and entrepreneur James Hogan made plans to build a libertarian city in Honduras as a test ground for the Seasteading Institute's free-floating islands. They thought they had the approval of the government, only to find out that changing the constitution of a city wasn't all that easy. The two of them abandoned the project and moved back to California. Friedman left the Tortuga commune and moved up to Berkeley, where he met a tall, lithe redhead named Brit Benjamin. He decided to pivot to monogamy, and the two were engaged in 2015. He went back to work as an engineer at Google.

In later classes of fellows, the Thiel Fellowship program expanded to include anyone under twenty-two, rather than twenty, and required taking off only a year from college. To deal with the surge, and increased interest, Thiel hired a new leader named Jack Abraham. At the time, he was a little-known twenty-nine-year-old entrepreneur who had sold his local shopping engine to eBay in 2010 for $75 million.

Abraham, who looked more like he was nineteen, had short,

spiky hair, a round face, and a wide smile. He too had dropped out of college, and the thinking was that he would provide inspiration to the new classes of Thiel fellows.

Abraham grew up in northern Virginia, the son of an amateur artist mother who died of ovarian cancer when he was sixteen, and a father who was the CEO of a software analytics company valued currently at about $1 billion. He started working for his father at thirteen and then went on to the Wharton School. There he took computer science and business, and ultimately designed his own major. It was a typical path, until his senior year came along. Instead of applying to Wall Street or to a consulting firm, as most other business school grads were doing in 2008 when he graduated, he decided to start his own company.

It would be a local shopping search engine called Milo, but at the time, Abraham didn't have a plan, just a desire to do something on his own. "I just remember everyone was talking about Goldman Sachs, Bain Capital, and McKinsey," he said. "People just thought I was crazy that I wasn't going to these places." At the time, if you were interested in engineering, you'd go to Google. "Working at Google was like what working at Facebook or Twitter is today," he said.

So one semester before graduating from college, Abraham left for Silicon Valley. It took one trip out there to see that it was where he wanted to be. He rented a motel room in Palo Alto for the first two weeks and then finally found an apartment off

University Avenue that would double as an office. "I knew this was the center of technology," he said, remembering of the time: "We slept there and worked there and ate ramen—the classic story."

For the first few months, living in Palo Alto was a lonely existence. He had only one real friend there, his roommate and coworker. "It was pretty isolating," he recalled. The early Thiel fellows were also without cars or much means, and often found themselves trapped in their house on Santa Rita Street. Years later, when he became director of the program, no doubt his own experience sensitized Abraham to what many Thiel fellows were going through. However, the utter lack of a social life didn't prevent him from creating technology that enabled a function called eBay Now, which allowed customers to buy products from local stores on their phones. He also created a feed like the ones on Facebook and Twitter enabling eBay sellers to show customers what new products were available.

After two years there, he started a new company, Atomic Labs, billed as a "foundry" that also builds new companies. "It fits into the zero-to-one thesis," explained Abraham, referring to Peter Thiel's book of the same name, which promoted the idea that the best companies should be entirely new ideas rather than copies of existing inventions.

As director of the Thiel Fellowship, Abraham recently broadened the applicant pool because "great ideas can come at any point in your college career." He capped it at twenty-two, though, on account of the risk-aversion principle he found in those who had left to go to banks and consulting firms. There just wasn't enough incentive to be original.

The following year, 2015, thanks largely to the worldwide success of Thiel's *Zero to One* (a quarter million copies sold in the United States and a million in China), nearly 4,500 people applied, a 50 percent increase over the year before. Along with readers of the book, Abraham credited "entrepreneurial fever spreading across all the campuses" with the uptick. Kids were no longer going into investment banking and consulting as much anymore. They were eager to get into the tech world. There was a fear spreading that technology was taking over jobs. And a generation of graduates wanted to get there first—no matter that their quest may have been signaling the bubble's near burst.

In the end, the Thiel Fellowship was a microcosm of the millennial generation. It said, "If you're so good, let's take the best and brightest among you and see if you can prove it"—and maybe the fact that they didn't start billion-dollar companies didn't matter.

Maybe all that mattered was that the struggle of starting anew and being alone was so foreign to this generation that even Silicon Valley shimmer couldn't overcome it. Thiel's program was a blank slate. It was a new glimpse into adolescence and young adulthood air-dropped into the context of the most successful sector in the country.

Where were the Thomas Jeffersons and Alexander Hamiltons who started a country from nothing? Who were these people who actually did start companies? For those who had been anointed, what did the network really do for them? What was success? Were these companies even successful?

What was definitively a success about the fellowship was its very idea: the idea of breaking away from what an institution enforced and had to be. Since the Thiel program started, the idea of going to college wasn't as necessary as it used to be. People who dropped out or skipped it all together were often considered more talented, and were perceived to have the potential to be even more of a prodigy. They must have been up to something original, suggested the new consensus.

It also helped change what a job was supposed to be. Instead of becoming a lawyer or doctor, the greater currency was doing something you wanted to. Just as the idea of romantic love changed marriage from a duty to something you were supposed to be passionate about, Silicon Valley changed work from something that was a routine part of life in order to make money and support a family, to something that was now expected to be exhilarating and fun.

Today, in certain sectors of society, work is supposed to be like play. It's partly because Google built an office to look like a big playroom, as did Apple and Facebook. At work, you weren't supposed to grow into a serious adult but become more childlike, have a better time, be happier, more mindful. The workday had become like recess.

The Thiel fellows were examples of today's kids who felt too smart to just go to a bank or a law firm or some other plebeian place where regular graduates went. No, talent went west these days, and if schools couldn't help with that, what were they there for? Now schools all around the country offered entrepreneurial programs and classes on how to found a start-up. Cities were building tech centers and trying to replicate Stanford as best they could. The Harvard Innovation Lab, I-Lab, looked like a mini Google, nestled next to the university's ivy-covered business school.

Along with this migration came an even further push. Not only the superiority of the valley but the superiority of what it made: the machine.

The fear that technology was outpacing humans was a strange derivative of natural selection and evolution. It was the idea that whatever was better would win, and in this case, it was the microchips. It naturally followed in evolution that the being with the superior capabilities would take over the race beneath it—in this case, humans.

Was it a denial of the humanities and the emotions, and the feeling one gets after grasping a deep meaning or falling in love or feeling something greater? How could a machine do that? In Silicon Valley, some people started saying that those enmeshed in artificial intelligence were developing a sort of different personality, one that was somewhat lacking in emotion—flatliners, in a way. They were strangely devoid of passion.

It was a new personality type on top of the networking one—which also was empty of real reactions. Humans, especially the Silicon Valley breed, didn't naturally network or talk to one another but instead almost programmed themselves to be social. They forced themselves to network and meet one another, much like machines interfacing.

The only problem was that artificial intelligence's promises were much like many of the inflated company valuations. The programs didn't quite work yet. The robots didn't really have emotion. They raised their eyebrows. They frowned. But they didn't feel. Or anything close to it. They had no personality.

Was a backlash coming? Was there no *there* there? It seemed like these kids were well positioned to find out. As Thiel fellow guinea pigs, they were the discoverers of what the myth held, at least for outsiders.

While some went back to the lives they knew, often with a greater appreciation of them, the others stayed out there in the new world where the fellowship had succeeded, at least as a thought experiment.

It made people question the establishment, and while the program may have come at a time that was too early for there to be an existing framework for kids who decided to skip school, what it did do was challenge political correctness and fly in the face of what academic institutions had previously made mandatory.

Most of the fellows became famous at least briefly, but they also got to be pioneers of a new frontier. Now there was another path, and the destination was far more open-ended than it ever had been before.

What the program also did was to reveal just what that took to make it in Silicon Valley. It exposed the gold rush to be a bit of a mirage in practice. The underbelly was so much bigger than the brain trust—where all the real profit and all the real genius sat.

Instead of copying the genius of some of these people—the original PayPal mafia, for example—young people were coming in droves to copy their peculiarities, their weirdness, their odd behavior, in hopes that some of it would rub off, and they'd become billionaires by association or by exercise. Achievement through emulation was far less successful than achievement through invention. Original thinking didn't derive from living in a group house or swearing off gluten with other founders. But they found out the hard way that being on an all-butter diet didn't make you a billionaire.

The young, aspiring entrepreneurs were seduced by the lifestyle, by the oddity of it all. They were the new waiters and waitresses on Sunset Boulevard trying to win Oscars in Hollywood.

And as more and more arrived, their behavior was beginning to mimic those of the East Coast, but instead of Nantucket reds, they wore sweatshirts. Instead of sailing sunfish, they rode Segways. There was the often not-so-hidden drive to make even more money than the people on the East Coast, who said they wanted to make money much more openly.

The stated Silicon Valley goal of "changing the world," a phrase that rang earnestly throughout the valley, had become a cliché. What was the noble cause? many of the kids wondered.

The people who succeeded there weren't the lemmings; they were, in some cases, the lucky ones, but most possessed brilliant minds. Peter Thiel was one of these rarities. He somehow attracted those unique people too, but even he couldn't necessarily create them. While the fellows could well go on to great things, what John Burnham got out of it was an appreciation of all that came before—and all that the Silicon Valley bubble had made him, and so many others, forget.

Acknowledgments

Thank you to Ben Loehnen at Simon & Schuster, who made *Valley of the Gods* exist. He provided more insights and observations than pages in this book.

Thank you to my agent, Sloan Harris, whose honesty and patience have been unmatched and invaluable. And many thanks to Alexander Gortman for his tireless research.

Peter Thiel inspired this book. He piqued my curiosity about Silicon Valley and about people who have the courage to think differently and then execute on their ideas. Peter introduced me to people more impressive and fascinating than I thought possible, some of whom I now count as my best friends, such as Nellie L., Stephen C., and Ted and Kathleen Janus. Thank you to Kirsten Bartok, whose generosity allowed me to report this book.

I'd also like to send a warm and enthusiastic thanks to my editors at the *Wall Street Journal*, namely Gary Rosen, Lisa Kalis, and Gerry Baker, who not only help run, in my biased opinion, the world's finest newspaper, but also the happiest, most exciting, and energetic place to work.

To Frank DiGiacomo, whose writing and perspective I will forever admire. To Richard Story, whose style and wit will always be what I aspire to have. And to the memory of Peter Kaplan for those hours in his office, in which every sentence relayed the zeitgeist and every reporter felt like a star.

Thank you to my friends Mark Colodny and Sara Clemence, who were kind and tolerant enough to read early versions of this book and immeasurably improve the next drafts. To Perri Peltz, whose friendship and example helped me weather waves of setback. And to Drew, who also thinks that "crazy is a compliment."

Finally, to my parents, who all of this is for, and all of it is from.

Some of the material in this book has been previously published in a different form in the magazines and newspapers I have been privileged to write for over the past few years. Sections of the prologue were adapted from my story "Mating in Silicon Valley," edited by Dana Brown, in *Vanity Fair*'s May 2013 issue. The Prologue and Chapter 4 contain sections from my articles for *Departures*, "Palo Alto's New Tech Barons" and "Silicon Valley's Stanford Connection," in the magazine's October 2011 and September 2012 issues, respectively. Thanks to the editors at *Marie Claire*, for whom I wrote "Valley Girls" in April 2013, and used material adapted in Chapter 3. Sections of Chapter 7 were previously included in *Condé Nast Portfolio* in "Never Say Die" in the magazine's December 2007 issue. Material in Chapter 12 was adapted from my columns on Ray Kurzweil and David Gelernter for the *Wall Street Journal* on May 30, 2014, and November 29, 2013, respectively, and material in Chapter 6 was adapted from my *Wall Street Journal* column on Laura Arrillaga-Andreessen that ran on September 5, 2013.

About the Author

Alexandra Wolfe is a staff reporter for the *Wall Street Journal* and writes the weekly column "Weekend Confidential." After graduating from Duke University, she worked as a staff reporter for the *New York Observer*, the *Wall Street Journal*, and then *Condé Nast Portfolio*. As a freelancer, she wrote regular columns for *Bloomberg Businessweek*, features for *Travel + Leisure* and *Departures*, and has written cover stories for *Vanity Fair* and *Town & Country*. *Valley of the Gods* is her first book.